# Lecture Notes in Economics and Mathematical Systems

For information about Vols. 1–49, please contact your bookseller or Springer-Verlag

Vol. 50: Unternehmensforschung Heute – Übersichtsvorträge der Züricher Tagung von SVOR und DGU, September 1970. Herausgegeben von M. Beckmann. IV, 133 Seiten. 1971.

Vol. 51: Digitale Simulation. Herausgegeben von K. Bauknecht und W. Nef. IV, 207 Seiten. 1971.

Vol. 52: Invariant Imbedding. Proceedings 1970. Edited by R. E. Bellman and E. D. Denman. IV, 148 pages. 1971.

Vol. 53: J. Rosenmüller, Kooperative Spiele und Märkte. III, 152 Seiten. 1971.

Vol. 54: C. C. von Weizsäcker, Steady State Capital Theory. III, 102 pages. 1971.

Vol. 55: P. A. V. B. Swamy, Statistical Inference in Random Coefficient Regression Models. VIII, 209 pages. 1971.

Vol. 56: Mohamed A. El-Hodiri, Constrained Extrema. Introduction to the Differentiable Case with Economic Applications. III, 130 pages. 1971.

Vol. 57: E. Freund, Zeitvariable Mehrgrößensysteme. VIII,160 Seiten. 1971.

Vol. 58: P. B. Hagelschuer, Theorie der linearen Dekomposition. VII, 191 Seiten. 1971.

Vol. 59: J. A. Hanson, Growth in Open Economies. V, 128 pages. 1971.

Vol. 60: H. Hauptmann, Schätz- und Kontrolltheorie in stetigen dynamischen Wirtschaftsmodellen. V, 104 Seiten. 1971.

Vol. 61: K. H. F. Meyer, Wartesysteme mit variabler Bearbeitungsrate. VII, 314 Seiten. 1971.

Vol. 62: W. Krelle u. G. Gabisch unter Mitarbeit von J. Burgermeister, Wachstumstheorie. VII, 223 Seiten. 1972.

Vol. 63: J. Kohlas, Monte Carlo Simulation im Operations Research. VI, 162 Seiten. 1972.

Vol. 64: P. Gessner u. K. Spremann, Optimierung in Funktionenräumen. IV, 120 Seiten. 1972.

Vol. 65: W. Everling, Exercises in Computer Systems Analysis. VIII, 184 pages. 1972.

Vol. 66: F. Bauer, P. Garabedian and D. Korn, Supercritical Wing Sections. V, 211 pages. 1972.

Vol. 67: I. V. Girsanov, Lectures on Mathematical Theory of Extremum Problems. V, 136 pages. 1972.

Vol. 68: J. Loeckx, Computability and Decidability. An Introduction for Students of Computer Science. VI, 76 pages. 1972.

Vol. 69: S. Ashour, Sequencing Theory. V, 133 pages. 1972.

Vol. 70: J. P. Brown, The Economic Effects of Floods. Investigations of a Stochastic Model of Rational Investment. Behavior in the Face of Floods. V, 87 pages. 1972.

Vol. 71: R. Henn und O. Opitz, Konsum- und Produktionstheorie II. V, 134 Seiten. 1972.

Vol. 72: T. P. Bagchi and J. G. C. Templeton, Numerical Methods in Markov Chains and Bulk Queues. XI, 89 pages. 1972.

Vol. 73: H. Kiendl, Suboptimale Regler mit abschnittweise linearer Struktur. VI, 146 Seiten. 1972.

Vol. 74: F. Pokropp, Aggregation von Produktionsfunktionen. VI, 107 Seiten. 1972.

Vol. 75: GI-Gesellschaft für Informatik e.V. Bericht Nr. 3. 1. Fachtagung über Programmiersprachen · München, 9.–11. März 1971. Herausgegeben im Auftrag der Gesellschaft für Informatik von H. Langmaack und M. Paul. VII, 280 Seiten. 1972.

Vol. 76: G. Fandel, Optimale Entscheidung bei mehrfacher Zielsetzung. II, 121 Seiten. 1972.

Vol. 77: A. Auslender, Problèmes de Minimax via l'Analyse Convexe et les Inégalités Variationelles: Théorie et Algorithmes. VII, 132 pages. 1972.

Vol. 78: GI-Gesellschaft für Informatik e.V. 2. Jahrestagung, Karlsruhe, 2.–4. Oktober 1972. Herausgegeben im Auftrag der Gesellschaft für Informatik von P. Deussen. XI, 576 Seiten. 1973.

Vol. 79: A. Berman, Cones, Matrices and Mathematical Programming. V, 96 pages. 1973.

Vol. 80: International Seminar on Trends in Mathematical Modelling, Venice, 13–18 December 1971. Edited by N. Hawkes. VI, 288 pages. 1973.

Vol. 81: Advanced Course on Software Engineering. Edited by F. L. Bauer. XII, 545 pages. 1973.

Vol. 82: R. Saeks, Resolution Space, Operators and Systems. X, 267 pages. 1973.

Vol. 83: NTG/GI-Gesellschaft für Informatik, Nachrichtentechnische Gesellschaft. Fachtagung „Cognitive Verfahren und Systeme", Hamburg, 11.–13. April 1973. Herausgegeben im Auftrag der NTG/GI von Th. Einsele, W. Giloi und H.-H. Nagel. VIII, 373 Seiten. 1973.

Vol. 84: A. V. Balakrishnan, Stochastic Differential Systems I. Filtering and Control. A Function Spaoe Approach. V, 252 pages. 1973.

Vol. 85: T. Page, Economics of Involuntary Transfers: A Unified Approach to Pollution and Congestion Externalities. XI, 159 pages. 1973.

Vol. 86: Symposium on the Theory of Scheduling and its Applications. Edited by S. E. Elmaghraby. VIII, 437 pages. 1973.

Vol. 87: G. F. Newell, Approximate Stochastic Behavior of n-Server Service Systems with Large n. VII, 118 pages. 1973.

Vol. 88: H. Steckhan, Güterströme in Netzen. VII, 134 Seiten. 1973.

Vol. 89: J. P. Wallace and A. Sherret, Estimation of Product. Attributes and Their Importances. V, 94 pages. 1973.

Vol. 90: J.-F. Richard, Posterior and Predictive Densities for Simultaneous Equation Models. VI, 226 pages. 1973.

Vol. 91: Th. Marschak and R. Selten, General Equilibrium with Price-Making Firms. XI, 246 pages. 1974.

Vol. 92: E. Dierker, Topological Methods in Walrasian Economics. IV, 130 pages. 1974.

Vol. 93: 4th IFAC/IFIP International Conference on Digital Computer Applications to Process Control, Part I. Zürich/Switzerland, March 19–22, 1974. Edited by M. Mansour and W. Schaufelberger. XVIII, 544 pages. 1974.

Vol. 94: 4th IFAC/IFIP International Conference on Digital Computer Applications to Process Control, Part II. Zürich/Switzerland, March 19–22, 1974. Edited by M. Mansour and W. Schaufelberger. XVIII, 546 pages. 1974.

Vol. 95: M. Zeleny, Linear Multiobjective Programming. X, 220 pages. 1974.

Vol. 96: O. Moeschlin, Zur Theorie von Neumannscher Wachstumsmodelle. XI, 115 Seiten. 1974.

Vol. 97: G. Schmidt, Über die Stabilität des einfachen Bedienungskanals. VII, 147 Seiten. 1974.

Vol. 98: Mathematical Methods in Queueing Theory. Proceedings 1973. Edited by A. B. Clarke. VII, 374 pages. 1974.

Vol. 99: Production Theory. Edited by W. Eichhorn, R. Henn, O. Opitz, and R. W. Shephard. VIII, 386 pages. 1974.

Vol. 100: B. S. Duran and P. L. Odell, Cluster Analysis. A Survey. VI, 137 pages. 1974.

continuation on page 165

# Lecture Notes in Economics and Mathematical Systems

Managing Editors: M. Beckmann and W. Krelle

200

# The Resource Sector in an Open Economy

With contributions by

K. Enders, E. Gerken, H. Herberg
N. Van Long, M. G. Porter, H. Siebert

Edited by Horst Siebert

Springer-Verlag
Berlin Heidelberg New York Tokyo 1984

**Editor**

Prof. Dr. Horst Siebert
Universität Mannheim, A 5 – Seminargebäude
D-6800 Mannheim 1, FRG

ISBN-13: 978-3-540-12700-0 e-ISBN-13: 978-3-642-46484-3
DOI: 10.1007/978-3-642-46484-3



2142/3140-543210

# Preface

> "... the economics of exhaustible assets presents a whole forest of intriguing problems."
>
> Harald Hotelling[1)]

The two energy price shocks in 1973/74 and 1979/80 have arosed interest in the new area of resource economics. The affluent societies of Europe, North America and Japan were confronted with the new scarcity paradigm of the "space ship earth" with only a limited supply of natural resources aboard whereas population is growing and the environment cannot accomodate the increasing volume of pollutants.

The problem of natural resource scarcity gives rise to the question how resource-dependent economies like European countries and Japan are affected by an increase in resource prices and how they can adjust to rising energy prices. The new paradigm also has focused new interest on the problem of the resource-extracting firm and of the resource-exporting country. The Hotelling revival of resource economics has given new importance to the behavior and to the policy issues of resource-exporting countries.

In this volume, some important economic problems of the resource-exporting country are addressed. In Chapter I, a survey on the impact of the resource sector on the economy is given in a comparative-static framework. Moreover, the allocation problem of a resource-exporting country is analyzed in an intertemporal context. Should the resource-rich country deplete its resources quickly or should the time profile of ex-

---

1) H. Hotelling (1931), The Economics of Exhaustible Resources, "The Journal of Political Economy", 39 (1931), 137-175.

traction be chosen in such a way that depletion is postponed? The notion of an optimal intertemporal depletion policy is a baseline for the taxation of natural resources. The resource-rich country should institutionalize such a taxation scheme that the long-run interest of the resource-rich country is taken into account. This issue is discussed in Chapter IV by Porter. The comparative-static allocation problem of how the resource sector affects the rest of the economy is taken up in Chapters II, III and V. Long (Chapter II) and Herberg and Enders (Chapter III) discuss how a resource boom influences the sectorial structure of the economy. Gerken (Chapter V) analyzes the reverse case how a fall in the world price of natural resources bears upon the economy of a resource-rich country.

The papers of this volume have been presented in a seminar of the research group (Sonderforschungsbereich 5) "Allocation Policy in a Market Economy" at the University of Mannheim, Federal Republic of Germany. The Sonderforschungsbereich is sponsored by the Deutsche Forschungsgemeinschaft and attempts to find an answer to the laws governing allocation in a mixed economy. What is the optimal division of labor between the private and the government sector? Among different regions and industries of a nation? Among different nations? How can one discriminate between competing uses of factors of production? What are the opportunity costs (or user costs) to use a resource or a commodity for a specific purpose? Which allocation problems arise for specific resources such as labor, capital, land, natural resources and the environment? Which mechanisms and rules steer the allocation among generations? Do externalities require new property rights or do they necessitate government intervention? Does government intervention cause distortions and misallocations?

I would like to thank M. Corden, L. Cox, M. Faber, A. V. Kneese, N. V. Long, H. K. Schneider and I. Walter for arising and enforcing my interest in natural resources. Financial support from the Deutsche Forschungsgemeinschaft is gratefully acknowledged. I am also grateful to my collaborators at the University of Mannheim F. Dudenhöffer, H. Gebauer, J. Keck, H. Meder, A. Meyer, A. Seubert, and S. Toussaint who always ask the stimulating questions. Finally, I would like to thank E. Dreyer and J. Schafranek for preparing the manuscript for publication and A. Seubert for addressing himself to the index.

Horst Siebert

## About the Authors

Klaus Enders is an economist in the department of economics at the University of Kiel, Institut für Theoretische Volkswirtschaftslehre, Olshausenstr. 40-60, 2300 Kiel 1, Federal Republic of Germany

Egbert Gerken is a senior staff member at the Institut für Volkswirtschaft an der Universität Kiel, Düsternbrooker Weg 120, 2300 Kiel, Federal Republic of Germany

Horst Herberg is Professor of Economics at the University of Kiel, Institut für Theoretische Volkswirtschaftslehre, Olshausenstr. 40-60, 2300 Kiel 1, Federal Republic of Germany

Ngo Van Long is Professor of Economics at the Australian National University, Department of Economics, Copland Building, G.P.O. Box 4, Canberra 2601, Australia

Michael G. Porter is Professor of Economics and Director of the Centre of Policy Studies at the Monash University, Clayton Victoria 3168, Australia

Horst Siebert is Professor of Economics and International Trade at the University of Mannheim, A 5, 6800 Mannheim, Federal Republic of Germany

Contents

# Allocation Policy in a Resource - Exporting Country

by

Horst Siebert*

## 1. The Role of Resource Exports

For a large number of the countries of this world, exports of natural resources account for a sizable percentage of their export value. This ratio surpasses 90 percent for some of the crude oil exporters like Nigeria, Algeria, Iraq and Saudi Arabia. Non-oil exporting countries also reach high ratios of resource exports to total exports, for instance 89,8 percent for Mauritania (iron ore, copper ore), 84,6 percent for Kiribati (phosphates), 78,2 percent for Jamaica (bauxite), and 64,2 percent for Niger (uranium). Table 1 shows the ratio of the value of resource exports to total export value for the resource-exporting countries of the world.

Whereas for some countries resource exports are negligible in relation to gross domestic product [USA 0,4 (1980); Federal Republic of Germany 0,7 (1980)], this ratio reaches a high percentage for the typical resource-exporting country: 90,8 percent for Saudi Arabia, 89,2 percent for Brunei, 57,4 percent for Libya, 39,5 percent for Liberia, 29 percent for Algeria and 25,2 percent for Guyana.

Since exports are so vital as a determinant of national economic performance and as a stimulation of economic development, the role of exports has played a major role in the theory of economic development (Herrick and Kindleberger 1983; Singer

* I appreciate helpful comments from A. Meyer, A. Seubert, and S. Toussaint.

Table 1 Ratio of the Value of Resource Exports to the Value of Total Exports of Selected Countries [1)]

| Country | Year | Percentage | Types of resources |
|---|---|---|---|
| 60 - 90 percent | | | |
| Angola | (1974) | 60,4 | Petroleum, iron ore |
| Liberia | (1978) | 62,7 | Iron ore, diamonds, rubber crude |
| Syrian Arab. Rep. | (1978) | 63,8 | Crude petroleum, phosphates |
| Venezuela | (1979) | 64,2 | Crude petroleum, natural gas, iron ore |
| Niger | (1976) | 64,2 | Uranium, thorium ore |
| Indonesia | (1980) | 67,6 | Crude petroleum, nickel ores, copper ores, tin ores |
| Congo | (1978) | 68,9 | Crude petroleum, lead ores, diamonds |
| Kuwait | (1978) | 76,6 | Crude petroleum, natural gas |
| Jamaica | (1980) | 78,2 | Bauxite |
| Kiribati | (1979) | 84,6 | Phosphates |
| Mauritania | (1976) | 89,8 | Iron ore, copper ores |
| More than 90 percent | | | |
| Nigeria | (1978) | 90,0 | Crude petroleum, tin ores |
| Iran | (1977) | 92,4 | Crude petroleum, natural gas |
| Algeria | (1979) | 92,8 | Crude petroleum, natural gas |
| Qatar | (1979) | 93,8 | Crude petroleum |
| Libyan Arab Rep. | (1979) | 94,6 | Crude petroleum, natural gas |
| Brunei | (1978) | 95,9 | Crude petroleum |
| Saudi Arabia | (1980) | 96,7 | Crude petroleum, natural gas |
| Iraq | (1978) | 98,1 | Crude petroleum |
| United Arab Emir. | (1978) | 98,6 | Crude petroleum, natural gas |

1) Source: Tables No. 2 "Exports by industrial origins (percentage of total value)" and No. 5 "Special exports f.o.b. by commodities according to the S.I.C.T in thousand U.S. Dollars" in: United Nations (Ed.), 1980 Yearbook of International Trade Statistics, Vol. 1, New York 1981

and Ansari 1977), in trade theory (North 1955; Vernon 1966), in the debate on the terms of trade (Bhagwati 1958; Prebisch 1964; Singer 1950), in the discussion on stabilizing natural resource prices (MacBean 1966) and in trade policy issues (Corden 1974; Walter and Areskoug 1981).

## 2. The Impact of the Resource Sector on the Economy

In the typical resource - exporting country the resource sector affects the national economy through a network of interactions. The following effects can be distinguished.

Employment Effect. The resource sector will employ labor; and it may also provide an incentive to build capital internally. Very often, foreign capital is brought in.

Productivity Effect. In some developing countries the training of labor in the resource sector may be important. Similarly, the productivity of management may increase and technical knowledge may be brought into the country by the resource industry. Thus, the resource sector may be a vehicle of technology transfer.

Withdrawal Effect. Labor and capital have to be withdrawn from other sectors of the economy except when capital is imported from abroad. This withdrawal effect implies a reduction of output in the other sectors (agriculture, industry, service sector).

Linkage Effects. The resource sector may be interlinked with the other sectors of the resource country via backward and forward linkages (Hirschman 1957). The resource sector then can be conceived as a "firme motrice" (Perroux 1961) stimulating intermediary producers (backward linkage) and activities using the resource as an input (forward linkage, policy of vertical integration).

Income Effect. Production in the resource sector creates national income.

Distribution Effect. The income may accrue to private households, to the firms or to the government. It may accrue to the resource country or it may be transferred abroad.

Expenditure Effect. The impact of the expenditure effect will depend on how the income is spent. It may be reinvested in the private sector and it may increase the capital stock of the country. It may be spent in consumption by private households or it may be spent by the government for consumptive or investive purposes. If consumption expenditures affect nationally produced goods, the impact will differ with respect to the sector for whose products the income is spent (tradable versus non-tradable sector; agricultural, industrial or service products). Finally, resource earnings may be used to import consumption or investment goods.

Price Effect. The resource sector also causes a number of price effects. These may be classified into the influence on commodity prices, wages and the exchange rate.

Commodity Price Effects. The resource sector influences the supply and demand conditions for the other sectors of the economy, for instance via the supply side (productivity and withdrawal effect) and the demand side (income and expenditure effect). The price of output in another sector may rise or it may fall.

Wage Rate Effect. The resource sector may be willing to pay a higher wage rate in order to attract qualified workers. Or the trade unions in the resource sector may push for higher wages. The higher wage in the resource sector will dissipate to other sectors of the economy, either through the labor market or through the bargaining of labor unions.

Exchange Rate Effect. The resource sector earns foreign currency. Ceteris paribus, this implies a revaluation of the home currency. A revaluation, however, means that the absolute price advantage of the other sectors of the economy (agriculture, industry) is reduced. Consequently, they will tend to export less. The resource sector has a negative impact on the other sectors of the economy via the revaluation of the exchange rate (Corden 1981).

Allocation Effect. The combination of the above mentioned effects results in a sectoral shift in the economy in favor of the resource sector.

## 3. Intertemporal Allocation

The effects discussed above become relevant in a context of a comparative - static analysis. The resource country is shocked by an increase or a decline of the resource price in the world market. How does the economy of the resource country adjust to this stimulus? And through which channels does the resource sector influence the rest of the economy?

### 3.1 Intertemporal Optimality

Besides the comparative - static analysis of a shock in the parameters of the resource country, an intertemporal point of view is relevant for the resource - exporting country. For a resource-rich country, a stock of a depletable natural resource represents an asset. Exporting the resource and depleting the stock earns foreign currency and allows imports. But at the same time the resource-rich country loses the option to export the resource in the future. What does the country get in exchange if it runs down its stock of a natural resource? Does the utility enjoyed by earning foreign currency and by importing today outweigh the utility lost by foregone uses of the resource in future periods? (Siebert 1981a, 1982a,b)

Extracting the resource today is only justified if the opportunity costs of extraction are balanced by the benefits from extracting the resource. For a resource-extracting country, the marginal benefit from extraction is determined by consumption for the present generation or by future consumption made possible from extraction today. The opportunity or user costs are given by the opportunities foregone if the resource is extracted today, i.e., if the resource cannot be used tomorrow. What is the optimal long-run strategy of extraction for a resource-rich country? Should the stock be depleted very "early in the game"? Or should some part of the stock be kept untapped? Which time profile of extraction should be chosen? Which factors influence the optimal use of a natural resource over time? (Siebert 1981a)

The resource - exporting country has to steer extraction over time in such a way that the marginal benefit from extraction equals the marginal user costs of extraction. It is not worthwhile to extract the resource when the user costs of extracting it are greater than the marginal benefit derived from extraction today. Then the asset "resource" should be left in the ground. On the other hand, if the marginal benefits of extracting the resource today are larger than the user costs, the resource should be extracted.

Some important factors operate towards a dèclining rate of extraction over time. Consider for instance the simple case where the resource is exported in order to import consumption goods. Since the user costs rise with the discount rate and since user costs must be equal to marginal benefits, the marginal benefits must rise over time. Assuming a social welfare function (with the usual properties), this implies a smaller quantity of imports. With a given import price, the import value is reduced over time; consequently, the export value has to decrease as well. If the demand for the resource export is not inelastic, the resource price will rise and quantity demanded will fall.

## 3.2 Factors Influencing Intertemporal Supply

The general principle of equating marginal benefits and marginal opportunity costs does not yet give precise answers to the question how a resource-rich country should steer its time profile of extraction. It is necessary to specify marginal present benefits and user costs. Both variables are influenced by a variety of phenomena.

Resource Endowment. A country may have an abundant or a scarce endowment of a natural resource. Abundance for example means that the country may have a large stock relative to the extraction rate so that a given rate of extraction can continue for many decades. It is apparent that a resource-exporting country with resource abundance in an intertemporal sense will supply large quantities today since the actual depletion of the resource stock has negligible user costs.

Capital Scarcity. Resource extraction is capital-intensive. The resource-exporting country may lack the capital to start a natural resource industry. The capital stock may be financed by internal savings; it may also be financed externally by borrowing in the international market or by bringing in foreign firms. In the case of oil, some countries have obtained capital stocks by redefining the property rights for extraction. The way in which the capital stock for extraction is financed has implications for the time profile of extraction.

Technological Gap. As a rule, the resource-exporting country does not have the technological knowledge to explore and extract the resource. It therefore has to bring in the technology from abroad. This can be done by a set of different measures such as granting extraction leases to international firms or buying their technological services. The transfer of technology is influenced by the institutional setting regulating extraction.

Discount Rate (Time Horizon). A high time preference favors an early extraction. The time preference rate of a resource-exporting country is influenced by such phenomena as individual and social attitudes towards the future, the functioning of the capital market, and the influence of the political system on the discount rate. For instance, the target function of a ruling family (class) in a resource - exporting country may determine the time preference rate of a country.

Elasticity of Import Demand. A resource-exporting country may be very dependent on its imports. This can be due to many factors such as an international demonstration effect in consumption (Nurkse 1953), the unwillingness or the impossibility to reduce import demand, or the necessity to import capital goods for national development. A low elasticity of import demand creates a pressure to earn foreign currency and to export resources. A low elasticity of import demand implies a large supply in present periods and a neglect of user costs.

Population. A large population in a country can be one reason for a low elasticity of import demand; a large population may make it difficult to build up capital internally requiring a high volume of imports for consumption. Resource exports become necessary in order to earn foreign currency.

Elasticity of Resource Demand. The time profile of extraction is also influenced by the demand for the resource. If the demand for the resource is inelastic, the resource-exporting country may have the option to increase its actual benefits by keeping the supply quantities small. If demand is elastic, this option is not available.

Political Response in Resource-Importing Countries. The elasticity of resource demand is affected by the political reaction in the resource-importing countries. If the political system in the industrial nations does not allow the market to react to price changes (compare the U.S. energy policy in the seventies), the price margin for the resource-exporting country may be increased. To let the market operate, implies to increase the long-run elasticity of demand, to stimulate substitution and to reduce resource imports.

Backstop Technology. The resource-exporting country is faced with the risk that the resource-importing countries may find a backstop technology (Nordhaus 1973) that reduces the value of its reserves or even makes them worthless. A backstop technology puts an upper limit on the resource price; it can also be interpreted as increasing the elasticity of demand of the resource-importing countries.

Competitive Position. Demand for a country's resource is also influenced by the country's position as a supplier in the world market. If a country dominates the market or if it can be considered to be a barometric price leader, it has some leeway to realize its own pattern of extraction. If, however, the country has to take into consideration the response of other suppliers, it is restricted in the extraction strategy.

Both, the comparative-static and the intertemporal allocation issue represent interlinked problems and should be studied simultaneously. The results of comparative - static analysis may be affected if the finite stock of natural resources is taken into account.

## 4. Some Policy Issues

In the real world, the following problems have developed for the resource-exporting countries.

The Dual Economy. Resource abundance of a country may not guarantee economic development. Bringing international mining firms into a developing country may raise the mining sector on a technological level comparable to international standards. But mining may not "carry over" to the rest of the economy, and the resource-rich country may have a "dual economy" (Hirschman 1957; Maull 1980): The export sector is operating on a high technological level, but the rest of the economy remains trapped in the pre-industrial stage. When the concept of the dual economy is applied to the world economy, the world may be conceived as following a polarizing pattern in which the agglomerated industrial nations grow and in which the periphery remains on a low level of development (Myrdal 1956; Predöhl 1962; Prebisch 1964).

The Dutch Disease. In a resource-exporting country, sectoral change and reallocation of factors of production takes place. In a resource boom, the resource sector will expand, attracting factors of production from the other sectors of the economy. Consequently, the other sectors of the economy will contract. This is especially true if the untradeable products of the economy (construction, service sector) are characterized by a high income elasticity of demand and a high labor intensity of production. Then the expansion of the resource-sector implies a contraction of the industrial sector. This problem has been denoted as the Gregory-effect (Gregory 1976) or the "Dutch disease" (Corden and Neary 1982; Hoel 1981; Long 1981). The problem is discussed in Chapter II by Long and in Chapter III by Herberg and Enders.

The de-industrialization[2] resulting from a resource boom can be considered as a normal adjustment process. From an intertemporal point of view, preventing the contraction of the industrial sector by policy intervention can only be justified if the de-industrialization is a temporary phenomenon with the industrial sector expanding when the resource boom is over. Then, high adjustment costs can be prevented by protecting the industrial sector. Only this argument of preventing adjustment costs can motivate why the resource boom can be interpreted as a "disease". Of course, one has to take into consideration that in the political process the protection of the industrial sector may evolve as a target in itself. Moreover, the scope of sectoral change is reduced when the inflow of foreign capital is allowed and when the participation rate of the labor force is increased (or when foreign workers are brought in).

Falling Resource Price. A case analogous to the Dutch disease arises when there is a depression in the international market of a resource and when the price of the exportable of a resource-country falls. For instance, the drop of copper prices in 1974/75 had a strong impact on the economy of Chile where copper exports accounted for 77 % of total export value in 1970 and about 50 % from 1975 on. The temporary change in copper prices implies a sectorial readjustment, i.e., a decline of the export sector and an expansion of the non-export sector. Similarly as in the case of the Dutch disease, the problem arises whether policy intervention can smoothen the adjustment process or whether adjustment should be postponed until the price drop in the international market stops. This issue is taken up by Gerken in Chapter V.

White Elephants. To accumulate capital at home, to attract

---

2) On the problem of de-industrialization compare F. Blackaby (1981).

industry and to locate industrial activities on a higher stage in the hierarchy of production (vertical integration) is a long-run policy option of the resource country. An important prerequisite of such a strategy is not to overestimate the internal rate of return of the investments. White elephants in the desert seem to be an issue for low absorbers, especially the Middle East countries.

Too Low Prices at Home. Quite a few resource-exporting countries have lower internal resource prices than in the world market, for instance Indonesia, Mexico and Venezuela in the case of petroleum products. One argument for this approach is to stimulate industrial development at home. If lower resource prices apply to the industrial sector only, the target of stimulating the home industrial base may be reached. Consider, however, the case in which the lower resource price at home is obtained through an export tax. Then, if households also use the resource extensively, the excess supply of the resource will be reduced in the process of economic development. The resource-rich country will decimate its export potential. This seems to be a problem for Indonesia, Mexico and Venezuela where it is politically very difficult to increase the price of gas in order to reduce home demand and increase export supply.

Too Much Foreign Debt. A country may be overexposed to international debt. High interest rates, falling resource prices and a high political time preference (with national elections in sight) may aggravate the debt situation. The country has to supply a large quantity of resource exports in order to pay its debt service. Its terms of trade will deteriorate. A devaluation of the home currency is required in order to reduce import demand and put aside foreign currency for the repayment of debt. Preventing capital outflow by limiting capital mobility may have a negative feedback on attracting capital in the future and on restructuring the existing debt.

Too High Government Spending. The volatility of resource prices seems to suggest that a resource-exporting country cannot rely with certainty on a constant amount of resource earnings in each period. This is especially true when government revenue largely depends on resource earnings. When government expenditures are relatively fixed, the country may be forced to export more resources with falling prices (inverse supply behaviour). In order to prevent such a situation, it is recommendable to distinguish among a transitory and a permanent component in the government spending of resource earnings.

Optimal Depletion. The resource-exporting country is faced with the problem of choosing an optimal pattern of extraction. Eventually, the stock of a non-renewable resource will be depleted. Depletion occurs too early when the country could have improved its welfare by postponing some extraction. Depletion occurs too late when the country has an untapped stock of a resource in a situation in which substitutes or powerful competitors depress the price of the resource.

Optimal Taxation. When extraction is undertaken by private firms, the optimal pattern of extraction is steered by the institutional setting for extraction (extraction licences) and by taxation. The resource country has to induce private firms to explore its natural resources and thus has to provide incentives for exploration and the attraction of foreign capital. At the same time, the resource country wants some benefits for depleting its natural assets; the country wants to capture part of the resource profits. This issue is taken up by Porter with respect to the Australian experience (Chapter IV). The asymmetry of the bargaining situation (Palmer 1980) between the resource country and the private firm is a crucial condition: Before the resource has been found, the private firm has the exploration risk, and the resource country has to grant favorable tax conditions to the private firms. When the resource has been found and profits arise, the original risk is forgotten and the bargaining position of the private firm is weakened considerably.

References:


Bhagwati, J. (1958), Immiserizing Growth: A Geometrical Note, Review of Economic Studies 25 (1957-1958), 201-205.

Blackaby, F. (Ed.) (1978), De-industrialization, London: Heinemann.

Brown, G. M. and Field, B.C. (1978), Implications of Alternative Measures of Natural Resource Scarcity, The Journal of Political Economy 86, 229-243.

Corden, W. M. (1974), Trade Policy and Economic Welfare, Oxford: Clarendon.

Corden, W. M. (1981), Exchange Rate Policy and the Resources Boom, The Australian National University Centre for Economic Policy Research, Discussion Paper, Canberra.

Corden, W. M. and Neary, P. (1982), Booming Sector and De-industrialization in a Small Open Economy, Economic Journal 92, 825-848.

Gregory, R. G. (1976), Some Implications of the Growth of the Mineral Sector, Australian Journal of Agricultural Economics 20, 71-91.

Herrick, B. and Kindleberger, C. P. (1983), Economic Development, 4th Ed., New York: McGraw-Hill.

Hirschman, A. O. (1957), Investment Policies and "Dualism" in Underdeveloped Countries, American Economic Review 47, 550-570.

Hoel, M. (1981), Employment Effects of an Increased Oil Price in an Economy with Short-Run Labour Immobility, Scandinavian Journal of Economics 83, 269-276.

Long, N. V. (1981), The Effects of a Booming Export Industry on the Rest of the Economy, Mimeographed, Australian National University.

MacBean, A. (1966), Export Instability and Economic Development, London: Allen and Unwin.

Maull, H. (1980), Europe and World Energy, London: Butterworth.

Myrdal, G. (1956), An International Economy. Problems and Prospects, New York: Harper.

Nordhaus, W. D. (1973), The Allocation of Energy Resources, Brookings Papers on Economic Activity, 529-576.

North, D. C. (1955), Location Theory and Regional Economic Growth, Journal of Political Economy 63, 243-258.

Nurkse, R. (1953), Problems of Capital Formation in Underdeveloped Countries, 2nd Ed., Oxford: Blackwell.

Palmer, K. F. (1980), Mineral Taxation Policies in Developing Countries: An Application of Resource Rent Tax, IMF Staff Papers 27, 517-542.

Perroux, F. (1961), La Firme Motrice dans la Région et la Région Motrice, Actes du Colloque International de l'Institut de Science Economique et l'Université de Liège, Brussels, 257-305.

Prebisch, R. (1964), Toward a New Trade Policy for Development, Repub. by the Secretary General of UNCTAD, New York: United Nations.

Predöhl, A. (1962), Das Ende der Weltwirtschaftskrise, Hamburg: Rowohlt.

Siebert, H. (1981a), The Intertemporal Supply of Natural Resources and the Recycling of Hotelling Rents. The Case of the Saudis, Discussion Paper, Mannheim.

Siebert, H. (1981b), Import Taxes and the Intertemporal Supply of Natural Resources, Discussion Paper, Mannheim.

Siebert, H. (1981c), Extraction of Natural Resources with Induced Changes in the Interest Rate, Discussion Paper, Mannheim.

Siebert, H. (1982a), The Intertemporal Supply of a Resource-Exporting Country with Internal Capital Accumulation, Discussion Paper, Mannheim.

Siebert, H. (1982b), Borrowing and Resource-Extraction of the Capital-Poor Country, Discussion Paper, Mannheim.

Siebert, H. (1982c), Optimal Taxation in a Resource-Exporting Country, Discussion Paper, Mannheim.

Siebert, H. (1983a), Ökonomische Theorie natürlicher Ressourcen, Tübingen: Mohr/Siebeck.

Siebert, H. (1983b), The Economics of Large-Scale Ventures, in: D. W. Pearce, H. Siebert and I. Walter (Eds.), Risks and the Political Economy of Resource Development, London: Mac Millan, chapter 2.

Singer, H. W. (1950), The Distribution of Gains between Investing and Borrowing Countries, American Economic Review 40, Papers and Proceedings, 473-485.

Singer, H. W. and Ansari, J. A. (1977), Rich and Poor Countries, 2nd Ed., London: Allen and Unwin.

Vernon, R. (1966), International Investment and International Trade in the Product Cycle, Quarterly Journal of Economics 80, 190-207.

Walter, I. and Areskoug, K. (1981), International Economics, 3rd Ed., New York: Wiley.

# On the Short-Run and Long-Run Effects of a Resource Boom

by

Ngo Van Long

## 1. Introduction

It is a commonly accepted proposition that a resource boom typically leads to a contraction of manufacturing output, at least in the short-run. This phenomenon, often referred to as the "Dutch Disease" or "de-industrialization", has been studied extensively in the literature.[1] The purpose of the present paper is to contribute to the ongoing process of development of the theory of the Dutch Disease by systematically isolating the various short-run mechanisms which lead to the contraction of manufacturing output (including the real-wage inflexibility mechanism, which is often neglected) and to show how the short-run effects may be reversed in the long-run. The various angles from which long-run effects may be studied are also identified.

The paper is organized as follows: In Section 2 some possible causes of a resource boom are discussed. The short-run effects of a resource boom are considered in Section 3, where different mechanisms are identified. Section 4 discusses the concept of the long run in the context of a resource boom and studies some possible long-run effects of the boom on outputs and relative prices.

---

1) See, for example, Gregory, R.G. (1976), Snape, R.H. (1977), Long, N.V. (1981), Corden, W.M. and Neary, P. (1982), Neary, P. and Purvis, D. (1981), Hoel, M. (1981), Herberg, H. and Enders, K. (1982).

## 2. Possible Causes of a Resource Boom

Existing models, while referring to increases in output of an exhaustible resource such as oil or natural gas, typically treat the resource boom as a permanent increase in the productivity of the resource industry, without regard to exhaustibility and to inter-temporal maximizing behaviour of resource firms. While this approach may be justified as a simplification to facilitate the analysis, it seems desirable to have a closer look at the micro-economic foundation of a "resource boom".

Several authors associate a resource boom with new substantial discovery of resource deposits. Intuitively, given any expected price path of the resource goods, firms which find themselves in possession of larger resource stocks will find it profitable to increase its current rate of extraction, provided that marginal extraction cost is an increasing function of the rate of extraction. This intuitively plausible assertion is proved below.

Consider a firm with an initial deposit $R_o$. Let $q(t)$ denote the rate of extraction and $C(q)$ the extraction cost. Given an expected price path $p(t)$, the task of the firm is to

$$\text{(P.1)} \quad \underset{q}{\text{Maximize}} \int_o^\infty [p(t)q(t) - C(q(t))]\, e^{-rt}\, dt \tag{2.1}$$

$$\text{subject to} \quad \int_o^\infty q(t)\, dt = R_o. \tag{2.2}$$

Among the necessary conditions for an optimal extraction path, we have

$$p(0) - C'(q(0)) = \psi(0), \tag{2.3}$$

$$\dot{\psi}(t) = r\psi(t), \tag{2.4}$$

where $\psi(t)$ is the shadow price of the resource deposit.

Now let $V(R_o)$ be the value of the maximized integral (2.1). It can be shown that $V(R_o)$ is a strictly concave function if $C(q)$ is strictly convex. It is also well-known that

$$V'(R_o) = \psi(0). \tag{2.5}$$

Using (2.4), (2.5) and the strict concavity of $V(R_o)$, we have

$$dq(0)/dR_o = -V''(R_o)/C''(q(0)) > 0. \tag{2.6}$$

This completes the proof of the proposition that a higher $R_o$ leads to a higher $q(0)$.

A resource boom, however, is not necessarily associated with new discoveries. An increase in the current price of the resource relative to the dicounted future price also leads to an increase in the current rate of extraction, provided the function $C(q)$ is strictly convex.

Formally, let $p_1(t)$ be the price path originally expected by producers, and $q_1(t)$ the extraction path which is optimal given that $p_1(t)$ is expected. Suppose that, for some reason, producers suddenly change their expectation from $p_1(t)$ to $p_2(t)$. The revised extraction path is $q_2(t)$. It can be shown that path $q_2(t)$ cuts path $q_1(t)$ from above if the difference $p_2(t)-p_1(t)$ rises at a rate less than the rate of interest.[2]

---

2) See Long, N.V. and Sinn, H.-W. (1982), where the case of constant cost is also considered.

## 3. Short-Run Effects of a Resource Boom

The "short-run" is typically characterized by the lack of response of a certain economic variable to an economic stimulus. The variable may be a quantity (for example, labour may not leave an industry immediately when the wage rate in that industry is lowered, because it takes time to find alternative employment); or a price (for example, in the short-run labour unions may insist on maintaining the real wage rate, but in the longer-run they may accept cuts in the real wage rate, having seen that the maintenance of a constant real wage rate entails reduced employment).

The number of possible short-run models which one may construct to study the effects of a resource boom is bewildering. Too often model builders, tempted by the desire to be "realistic", introduce many complicating factors which inevitably obscure the basic underlying mechanisms. In the present paper we wish to isolate the basic, essential factors. We will show that there are three basic and separate mechanisms by which a resource boom leads to industrial contraction in the short-run. These mechanisms are

(i) the transfer-equivalent mechanism,
(ii) the direct resource-pull mechanism, and
(iii) the real wage inflexibility mechanism.

We wish to show that each of these mechanisms can work <u>separately</u> and that each can produce short-run de-industrialization even in the absence of other mechanisms. In order to do this, we will develop a number of very simple models, each highlighting a single mechanism. We leave to the reader the task of integrating these simple models into a more general model.

## 3.1 Model 1: The Transfer-Equivalent Effect of a Resource Boom

In this sub-section we shall present a model which is an adaptation of Gregory (1976), but which is simpler in that the resource sector is assumed to be an export enclave, in the sense that it has no supply-side links with the rest of the economy.[3] We adopt the assumption of small country. The country consists of two sectors: the traded-goods sector and the non-traded goods sector. The non-traded goods sector produces goods and services that are not traded internationally: one thinks of housing, professional services, and the like. Traded goods, on the other hand, are goods for which there are perfect substitutes produced in foreign countries. Within the traded-goods sector, we assume that there are two sub-sectors: the traditional traded-goods sub-sector, which we shall call "manufacturing" for short, and the new booming resource-exporting sub-sector.

Let $P_R$, $P_M$, $P_N$ denote the nominal prices of resource goods, manufacturing and non-traded goods, respectively. The ratio $P_R/P_M$ is exogenously given, the country being small. The output of the resource sub-sector is denoted by $Q_R$. We shall restrict our attention to a small time interval $[t_o, t_o+dt]$, and assume that within this time interval all variables remain constant if there are no external shocks. A resource boom can be modelled either as an exogenous increase in $Q_R$ or as an unexpected improvement in the terms of trade, $P_R/P_M$. We shall restrict our attention to the former specification.

Given that the resource sub-sector is an export enclave, we can draw the transformation curve relating manufacturing output to the output of non-traded goods. We assume that this transformation curve has the usual concave shape, as illustrated in

3) In Gregory's model the supply of the resource goods depends on the relative price of non-traded goods, so that the resource sector is not an export enclave.

Figure 1. This assumption implies that at least one factor of production can move between manufacturing and the non-traded goods sector.

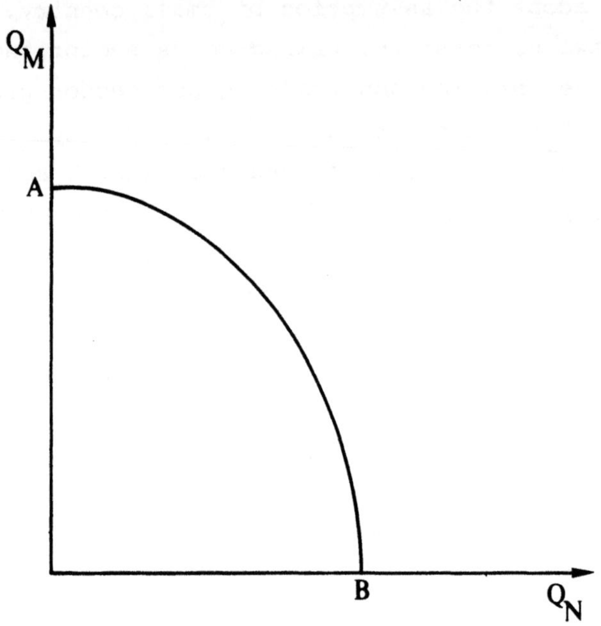


Figure 1

Defining the aggregate output of all traded goods as

$$Q_T = Q_M + (P_R/P_M)Q_R, \tag{3.1}$$

and the price of traded goods as

$$P_T = P_M, \tag{3.2}$$

we can draw the economy's production possibility curve, for a given $Q_R$, in the $(Q_N,Q_T)$ space, as in Figure 2, where the curve A'B' is obtained by shifting the curve AB in Figure 1 upwards by the vertical distance $(P_R/P_M)Q_R$.

Assume that initially the country is in equilibrium at point E in Figure 2, with income equal expenditure and zero excess demand in the non-traded goods market. A boom in the resource subsector is represented by an exogenous increase in $Q_R$, shifting A'B' upwards to the new position A"B". The vertical distance between A"B" and A'B' is $(P_R/P_M)\Delta Q_R$. At the old equilibrium price ratio, $P_N/P_M$, the new production point will be at F (vertically above E) while the new consumption demand point will be at C, north-east of E and south-east of F, provided that all income is spent and that the income elasticity of demand for non-traded goods is positive. There will be an excess demand for non-traded goods. Given that income equals expenditure, this excess demand for non-traded goods can only be eliminated by a rise in the relative price $P_N/P_M$, causing a contraction in manufacturing output and an expansion of the non-traded goods output (a movement from K to L in Figure 2).

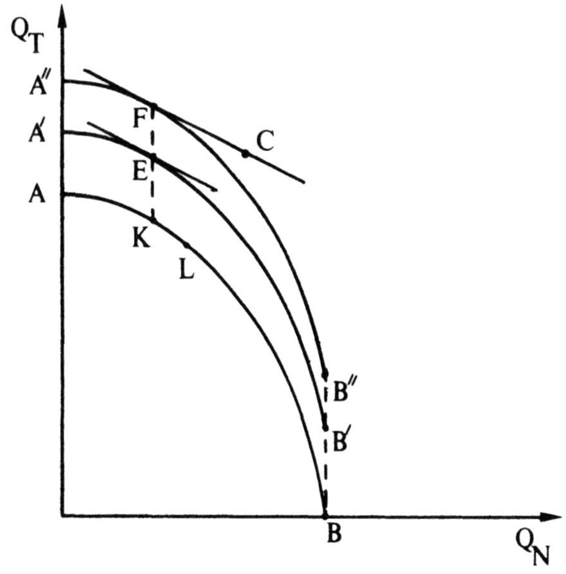


Figure 2

For simplicity we have assumed that income equals expenditure in the new equilibrium, in other words, that all the increase in income is spent on consumption goods. But that assumption is not necessary: as long as some of the increase in income is spent, the same qualitative result will be obtained. On the other hand, if all the additional income is used to accumulate wealth, then there is no change in consumption, output and relative price.

So far we have assumed that the boom takes the form of an increase in $Q_R$. Obviously, if the home country does not consume the resource good, then the effects of a $\theta$ per cent increase in $Q_R$ are identical to the effects of an increase in $P_R/P_M$ by the same percentage (with $Q_R$ constant). This equivalence does not hold if the home country consumes the resource good. In particular if the resource good is a complement of non-traded goods, then an export boom in the form of an exogenous increase in $P_R/P_M$ may lead to a fall in demand for non-traded goods and a rise in manufacturing output.

Another qualification to the results of Model 1 must be made: in developing the model we have adopted the simplifying assumption that non-traded goods are homogeneous. In reality there are many categories of non-traded goods, and their elasticities of substitution (in consumption) with respect to traded-goods may lie anywhere in the range $(0,\infty)$. Intuitively we may expect that a resource boom will tend to reduce the output of those non-traded goods for which imports are close substitutes - other things being equal. (These "other things" include income elasticities of demand and supply elasticities.)

To summarize, in Model 1 the resource boom is conceived of as equivalent to an increase in the foreign transfer received by the home country. The booming export sub-sector does not directly pull productive resources (factors of production) away from the manufacturing sub-sector. It only generates an increase in income which causes consumers to spend more on both traded and non-traded goods. While the increased demand for traded-goods can be satisfied by increased imports, the increased demand for non-traded goods must be met by diverting factors of production away from manufacturing.

## 3.2 Model 2: The Direct Resource-Pull Effect of an Export Boom

Model 2, which we shall consider in this sub-section, has two variants. The simplest version (Model 2.A) does not include non-traded goods, so as to highlight the direct resource pull effect of an export boom. In Model 2 the resource industry is is not an export enclave: it competes with manufacturing in the factor market.

In Model 2.A all goods are traded, so that the level and composition of demand in the home country is irrelevant as far as outputs of resource goods and of manufacturing are concerned. We assume that the production functions exhibit diminishing marginal products. Outputs are given by

$$Q_R = \theta F^R(L_R, K_R), \tag{3.3}$$

$$Q_M = F^M(L_M, K_M), \tag{3.4}$$

where K and L stand for capital and labour, and where $\theta$ is a shift parameter, an increase in $\theta$ representing a Hicks-neutral technical progress.

It is assumed that capital is industry-specific in the short-run, while labour is perfectly mobile, but total labour supply is fixed:

$$L_M + L_R = \bar{L}. \tag{3.5}$$

Clearly an exogenous increase in $\theta$ or in $P_R/P_M$ will cause the resource industry to demand more labour, causing a decline in the output of manufacturing. The real wage rate (in terms of manufacturing) will rise, and profitability in the manufacturing industry will fall.

A more complicated version is Model 2.B, which includes the non-traded goods sector, with a neo-classical production function

$$Q_N = F^N(L_N, K_N) \tag{3.6}$$

and where $K_N$ is also fixed in the short-run.[4] Equation (3.5) is replaced by

$$L_M + L_R + L_N = \bar{L}. \tag{3.7}$$

Assuming that in each industry the marginal product of labour is a decreasing function of labour input, we can construct the transformation curve in the space $(Q_N, Q_T)$, where $Q_T$ is the aggregate output of traded-goods, as defined by (3.1). Figure 3 illustrates the transformation curve. It can be shown that the curve is strictly concave. The slope of the curve gives the opportunity cost of non-traded goods in terms of traded goods.

4) Model 2.B differs slighly form Snape, R.H. (1977) in that marginal product of labour is not constant.

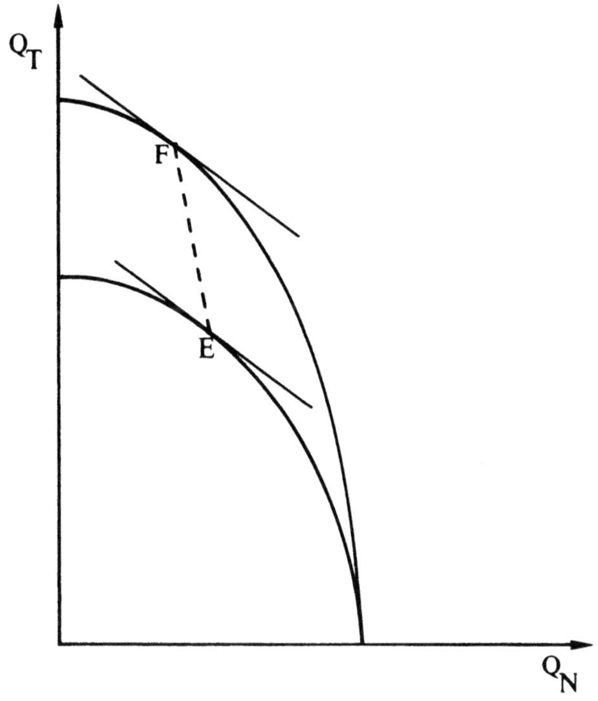


Figure 3

For a given $P_N/P_M$ a rise in $\theta$ will reduce supply $Q_N$ (from E to F), as an increase in $\theta$ (or in $P_R/P_M$) means that the opportunity cost of non-traded goods (at any given level of non-traded goods output) is higher than before. In other words the higher is $\theta$, the higher is the marginal cost curve (supply curve) of non-traded goods. On the demand side, an increase in $\theta$ will cause the demand curve for non-traded goods to shift upwards, via its effect on income. The new equilibrium price ratio $P_N/P_M$ must rise (see Figure 4), but the output $Q_N$ may rise or fall. The real wage rate (in terms of manufacturing) rises unambiguously because both the real marginal product curves ($MPL_T$ and $(P_N/P_M)MPL_N$) shift upwards, as illustrated in Figure 5. Employment in manufacturing must fall as a result of the real wage increase.

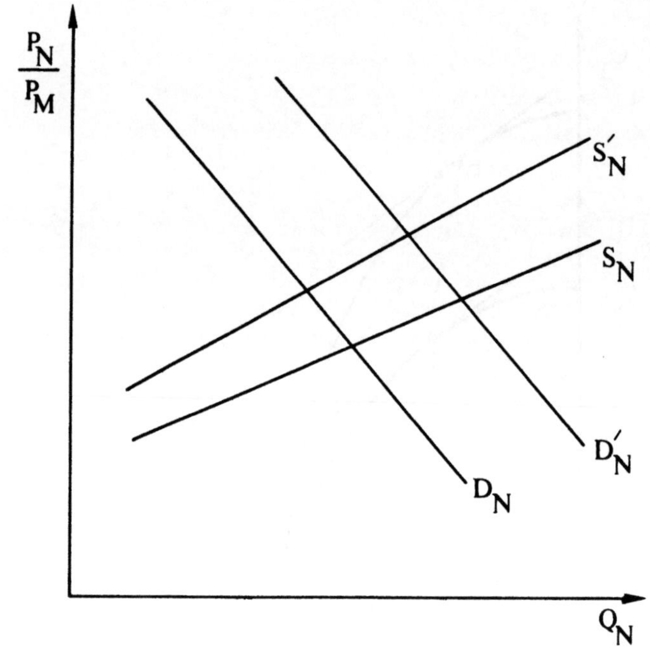


Figure 4

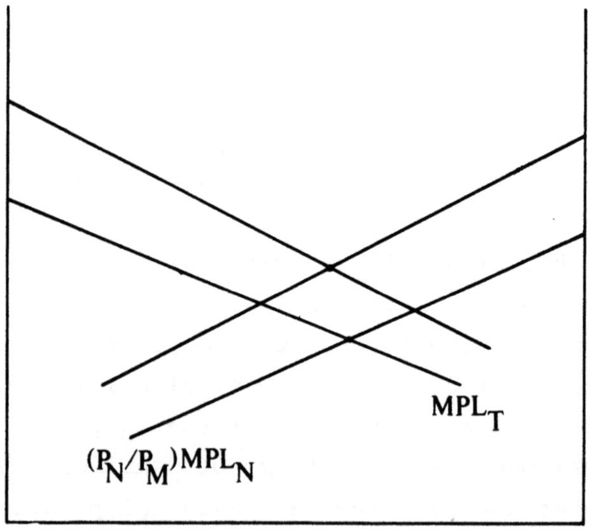


Figure 5

It should be noted that the above result does not rely on the assumption that income equals expenditure: As long as $P_N/P_M$ rises, the real wage rate (in terms of manufacturing) will rise, causing the manufacturing industry to reduce employment.

## 3.3 Model 3: Real Wage Inflexibility

In this sub-section we wish to show that an increase in the output of the resource sub-sector can lead to a contraction of manufacturing output without a direct resource-pull effect (as in Model 2) and without a movement of factors of production into the non-traded goods sector (as in Model 1).

We shall develop two versions of Model 3. In Model 3.A we assume that all factors of production are industry-specific. This assumption helps isolate the real-wage inflexibility effect from the transfer-equivalent effect of Model 1 and the direct resource-pull effect of Model 2. The assumption that all factors are industry-specific is perhaps too rigid. For this reason we shall also develop Model 3.B which allows some degree of factor mobility. The results of Model 3.B are richer. In particular we shall show that total employment may rise or fall even if real wage rate is inflexible.

### Model 3.A:

We assume that production functions are given by (3.3), (3.4) and (3.6). It is also assumed that the real rewards of all factors of production (except labour in manufacturing) are competitively determined, so that in equilibrium all factors (except $L_M$) are fully employed. Thus we can write

$$L_R = \bar{L}_R, \quad L_N = \bar{L}_N,$$

$$K_R = \bar{K}_R, \quad K_N = \bar{K}_N, \quad K_M = \bar{K}_M,$$

$$Q_N = \bar{Q}_N = F^N(\bar{L}_N,\bar{K}_N), \quad Q_R = \theta F^R(\bar{L}_R,\bar{K}_R).$$

As the real wage rate of $L_M$ is rigid, unemployment is possible

$$L_M \leq \bar{L}_M.$$

Let $W_M$ denote the nominal wage rate in manufacturing and let I be a cost-of-living index, which is positive, linear homogeneous and increasing function of all commodity prices:

$$I = G(P_N,P_R,P_M). \tag{3.8}$$

The real wage rate of labour in manufacturing, defined as

$$\tilde{W}_M = W_M/I, \tag{3.9}$$

is institutionally fixed. Since the function G is homogeneous of degree 1, we can write

$$I/P_M = G(E,T,1), \tag{3.10}$$

where

$$E \equiv P_N/P_M, \tag{3.11}$$

and

$$T \equiv P_R/P_M. \tag{3.12}$$

(To aid memory, one may think that T stands for "terms of trade" and E for the "real exchange rate".)

The demand for labour in manufacturing is given by the following equation:

$$F_1^M(L_M^D, \bar{K}_M) = W_M^*, \qquad (3.13)$$

where $W_M^*$ is defined as the real wage rate <u>in terms</u> of the manufacturing good:

$$W_M^* \equiv W_M/P_M, \qquad (3.14)$$

From (3.9), (3.10) and (3. 4)

$$W_M^* \equiv (W_M/I)(I/P_M) = \tilde{W}_M G(E,T,1). \qquad (3.15)$$

Since $\tilde{W}_M$ is assumed to be institutionally fixed, any increase in E or in T will result in an increase in $W_M^*$ and hence a reduction in the demand for labour in the manufacturing industry. For any given T, the functional relationship between $L_M^D$ and E, obtained from (3.13) and (3.15), is written as

$$L_M^D = L_M^D[W_M^*(E)]. \qquad (3.16)$$

We note that the elasticity of $W_M^*$ with respect to E is identical to the elasticity of the cost-of-living index with respect to $P_N$:

$$(E/W_M^*)(dW_M^*/dE) = (E\tilde{W}_M/W_M^*)\partial G(E,T,1)/\partial E$$

$$= [E/G(E,T,1)][\partial G(E,T,1)/\partial E]$$

$$= (P_N/I)(\partial I/\partial P_N) \equiv b_N. \qquad (3.17)$$

To summarize our results so far, we state the following proposition:

Proposition 1: Given the world price ratio $P_R/P_M$, an export boom represented by an increase in $\theta$ will lead to a fall in output and employment in manufacturing if and only if a rise in $\theta$ causes the price ratio $P_N/P_M$ to rise.

It remains to determine whether an increase in $\theta$ leads to an increase in $P_N/P_M$. To this end we specify the demand function

$$C_N = D^N(P_N, P_R, P_M, Y), \qquad (3.18)$$

where Y denotes nominal expenditure. The function $D^N$ being homogeneous of degree zero, we can re-write (3.18) as

$$C_N = D_N(E, T, 1, Z), \qquad (3.19)$$

where Z is real expenditure in terms of the manufacturing goods:

$$Z = Y/P_M. \qquad (3.20)$$

Define real income in terms of manufacturing goods as

$$V = F^M(L_M^D, \bar{K}_M) + E\bar{Q}_N + T\theta F^R(\bar{L}_R, \bar{K}_R). \qquad (3.21)$$

We assume that real expenditure is a function of real income[5]:

$$Z = f(V), \quad 1 \geq f'(V) \geq 0. \qquad (3.22)$$

5) Note that if the non-traded goods market is in equilibrium, the excess of income over expenditure is exactly equal to the balance of trade surplus. Since we are dealing with the short-run, we do not require that the balance of trade be in equilibrium.

Finally, we assume that the market for non-traded goods is cleared:

$$\bar{Q}_N = D^N(E,T,1,Z). \tag{3.23}$$

The system of equations (3.21), (3.22), (3.23) and (3.16) determine the short-run equilibrium values Z,V,E and $L_M^D$. To determine the effects of an increase in θ, we totally differentiate the above equations. From (3.16),

$$\hat{L}_M^D = \varepsilon_M^L b_N \hat{E}, \tag{3.16'}$$

where $\varepsilon_M^L$ is the elasticity of labour demand with respect to $W_M^*$, $b_N$ is the elasticity of the cost-of-living index with respect to $P_N$, and the hat stands for the proportional rate of change ($\hat{E}$ = (dE)/E, etc.). Similarly from (3.21),

$$\hat{V} = \alpha_V^M \beta_M^L \hat{L}_M^D + \alpha_V^N \hat{E} + \alpha_V^R \hat{\theta}, \tag{3.21'}$$

where

$$\alpha_V^M \equiv Q_M/V, \quad \alpha_V^N \equiv EQ_N/V, \quad \alpha_V^R \equiv TQ_R/V,$$

$$\beta_M^L \equiv W_M^* L_M^P/Q_M.$$

From (3.22),

$$\hat{Z} = [f'(V)V/Z]\hat{V} \equiv \phi\hat{V}, \tag{3.22'}$$

where $\phi$ is the elasticity of real expenditure with respect to real income. Finally, from (3.23),

$$0 = \varepsilon_N^D \hat{E} + \eta_N \hat{Z}, \tag{3.23'}$$

where $\varepsilon_N^D$ is the uncompensated price elasticity of demand for non-traded goods and $\eta_N$ is the elasticity of demand for non-traded goods with respect to total expenditure, Z.

From the above equations,

$$\hat{E}/\hat{\theta} = \eta_N \, \phi \, \alpha_V^R / (-\mu), \tag{3.24}$$

where

$$\mu = \eta_N \, \phi \, \alpha_V^M \, \beta_M^L \, \varepsilon_M^L \, b_N + \left[\eta_N \, \phi \, \alpha_V^N + \varepsilon_N^D\right]. \tag{3.25}$$

The first term on the right-hand-side of (3.25) is negative provided non-traded goods are normal ($\eta_N > 0$), the term inside the square brackets is also negative because

$$\eta_N \, \phi \, \alpha_V^N = f'(V) \; \eta_N \, \alpha_Z^N \leq \eta_N \, \alpha_Z^N, \tag{3.26}$$

(where $\alpha_Z^N \equiv EC_N/Z$) and

$$\eta_N \, \alpha_Z^N + \varepsilon_N^D = \bar{\varepsilon}_N^D, \tag{3.27}$$

where the compensated elasticity of demand $\bar{\varepsilon}_N^D$ is negative. Thus, provided non-traded goods are normal and some of the increase in income is consumed ($\phi > 0$), an increase in $\theta$ will lead to an increase in $P_N/P_M$ (= E) and a fall in $Q_M$ and $L_M$.

It is also worth noting that the fall in manufacturing output is less than the rise in the real output (measured in units of manufacturing goods) of the resource sub-sector.

To summarize the results of Model 3.A, we state the following proposition:

Proposition 2: Under the assumptions of the present model, an increase in $\theta$ will lead to an increase in $P_N/P_M$ and a reduction in manufacturing output and employment. The fall in $Q_M$ is less than the rise in $TQ_R$.

Model 3.B:

In Model 3.A all factors are industry-specific. We now relax this assumption slightly by allowing perfect mobility of labour between manufacturing and the non-traded goods sector. Thus

$$L_M + L_N \leq \bar{L}_{MN}. \tag{3.28}$$

Let $W_{MN}$ be the nominal wage rate for labour in manufacturing and in non-traded goods, and let

$$\tilde{W} \equiv W_{MN}/I, \tag{3.29}$$

where I is defined by (3.9). Again we assume that $\tilde{W}$ is institutionally fixed. Let

$$W_N^* \equiv W_{MN}/P_N, \tag{3.30}$$

and

$$W_M^* \equiv W_{MN}/P_M = EW_N^*. \tag{3.31}$$

The demands for labour in manufacturing and in the non-traded goods sector are given by

$$F_1^M\left(L_M^D,\bar{K}_M\right) = W_M^*, \tag{3.32}$$

$$F_1^N\left(L_N^D,\bar{K}_N\right) = W_N^*. \tag{3.33}$$

Equations (3.14) - (3.23) are retained.

From (3.19) - (3.22),

$$\hat{C}_N = \varepsilon_N^D \hat{E} + \eta_N \hat{Z}, \tag{3.34}$$

$$\hat{Z} = \phi\left[\alpha_V^M \hat{Q}_M + \alpha_V^N \hat{Q}_N + \alpha_V^N \hat{E} + \alpha_V^R \hat{\theta}\right]. \tag{3.35}$$

Now since

$$\hat{Q}_M = \beta_M^L \hat{L}_M^D, \quad \hat{Q}_N = \beta_N^L \hat{L}_N^D, \tag{3.36}$$

where $\beta_N^L \equiv W_N^* L_N^D/Q_N$, and since

$$\hat{L}_M^D = \varepsilon_M^L b_N \hat{E}, \tag{3.37}$$

$$\hat{L}_N^D = \varepsilon_N^L \hat{W}_N^* = \varepsilon_N^L(\hat{W}_M^*-\hat{E}) = \varepsilon_N^L(b_N-1)\hat{E}, \tag{3.38}$$

we have from (3.34) - (3.38)

$$\hat{C}_N = \varepsilon_N^D \hat{E} + \eta_N \phi\left[\alpha_V^R \hat{\theta} + \alpha_V^N \hat{E} + \psi\hat{E}\right], \tag{3.39}$$

where

$$\psi \equiv \alpha_V^M \beta_M^L \varepsilon_M^L b_N + \alpha_V^N \beta_N^L \varepsilon_N^L(b_N-1). \tag{3.40}$$

Now $\varepsilon_N^D + \eta_N \phi \alpha_V^N$ is negative provided that non-traded goods are normal, by the argument which follows (3.25). Thus the general equilibrium demand curve for non-traded goods is downward sloping provided $\psi < 0$ and provided non-traded goods are normal. The supply curve for non-traded goods is given by

$$\hat{Q}_N = \alpha_V^N \beta_N^L \varepsilon_N^L (b_N - 1)\hat{E}. \tag{3.41}$$

From (3.39) and (3.41) the effects of an increase in $\theta$ can be illustrated by simple diagrams (Figures 6 and 7).

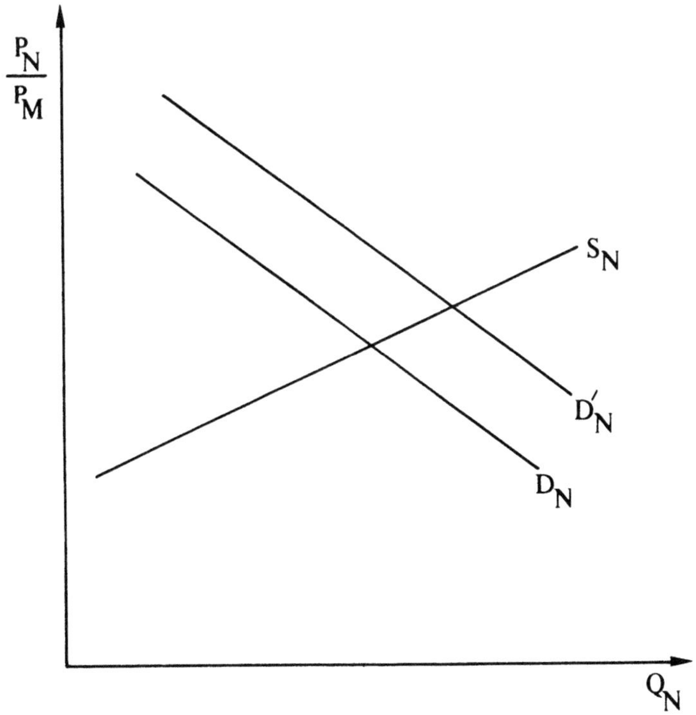


Figure 6

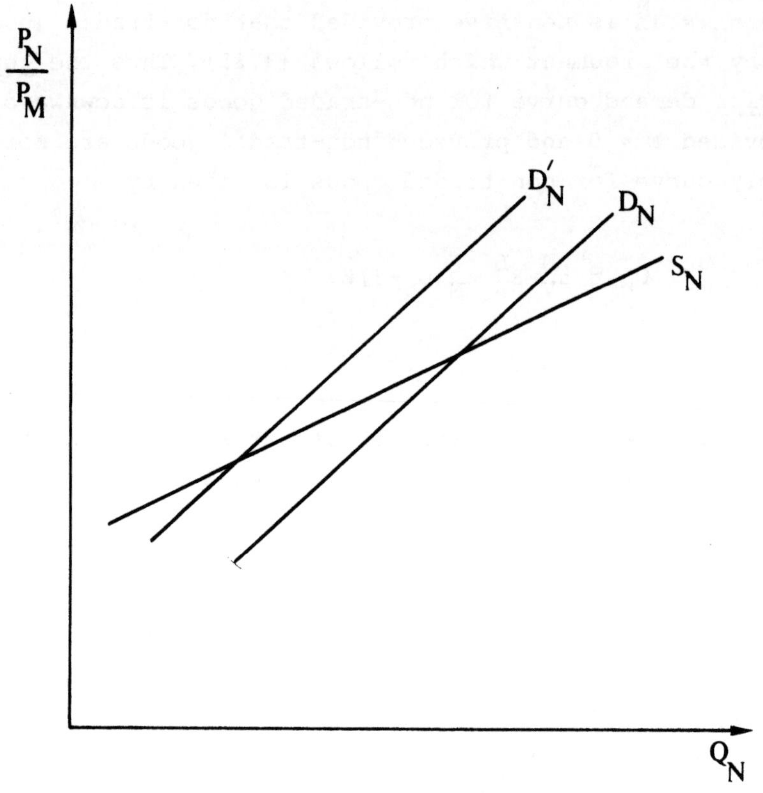


Figure 7

In Figure 6 we assume that non-traded goods are normal and that $\psi$ is negative. An increase in $\theta$ shifts the demand curve for non-traded goods upwards, resulting in a rise in both E and $Q_N$. (Note that the supply curve is not shifted.)

In Figure 7 we continue to assume that non-traded goods are not inferior (i.e. that $\eta_N > 0$), we also assume that $\psi > 0$. The latter assumption implies that any rise in E causes non-traded goods output to rise by more than the absolute fall in manufacturing output. In addition if $\eta_N > 1$, it is possible that the slope of the general equilibrium demand curve for non-traded goods, $\varepsilon_N^D + \eta_N \phi(\alpha_V^N+\psi)$, is steeper than the slope of the supply curve for $Q_N$, as given by (3.41). If this is the case, a rise in $\theta$, causing an upward shift in the demand curve, will result in a <u>fall</u> in the equilibrium values of E and $Q_N$ and hence a rise in $L_M^D$. This "paradoxical" result can be ruled out if we insist on Walrasian stability, for the situation depicted in Figure 7 is unstable: an excess demand will lead to a price increase which in turn causes a larger excess demand.

In the case depicted in Figure 6, any increase in $\theta$ will lead to higher employment in the non-traded goods industry and a fall in labour demand in manufacturing. The effect on total employment is ambiguous:

$$\hat{L}_{MN} = (L_M/L_{MN})\hat{L}_M + (L_N/L_{MN})\hat{L}_N$$

$$= \left[(L_M/L_{MN})\varepsilon_M^L b_N + (L_N/L_{MN})\varepsilon_N^L(b_N-1)\right]\hat{E}.$$

The effect on total employment is also ambiguous in the case depicted in Figure 7, where a rise in $\theta$ leads to higher employment in manufacturing and lower employment in the non-traded goods sector.

## 4. Some Long-Run Considerations

In the short-run models presented in Section 3, we assumed that the increase in income causes expenditure to rise, but not necessarily by the same amount. Presumably consumers may want to accumulate assets so as to achieve some long-run relationship between long-run income (including interest income) and financial wealth. For example, consumers may want to purchase foreign bonds so as to smooth out the time path of consumption. One possible specification of the asset accumulation rule is

$$\dot{B}(t) = \gamma[\kappa V(t)-B(t)], \quad \gamma > 0, \tag{4.1}$$

where V(t) is national income (output plus interest income from foreign bonds), and B(t) is the stock of foreign bonds held by the home country.

An alternative approach is to assume that consumers maximize an integral of discounted utility, subject to a budget constraint. For example,

$$\text{Max} \int_0^\infty U(C_1,C_2)e^{-\rho t}dt, \tag{4.2}$$

s.t.

$$\dot{B} = rB - \Sigma P_i C_i + \Sigma P_i Q_i, \tag{4.3}$$

$$\lim_{t\to\infty} B(t)e^{-rt} \geq 0. \tag{4.4}$$

Assume that all goods are traded, as in Model 2.A, and that technology is as specified in that model. The consumption decisions must satisfy the following necessary conditions

$$\hat{U}_i = \rho - [r-(\dot{P}_i/P_i)], \tag{4.5}$$

where $U_i$ is the marginal utility of $C_i$. Note that from (4.3), the balance of trade is given by

$$T = \Sigma P_i(Q_i-C_i) = \dot{B} - rB. \tag{4.6}$$

For a small country, production decisions are independent

of consumption decisions. If we rule out the accumulation of physical capital and assume a constant labour force, the value of aggregate output of a resource exporting economy will be falling over time provided prices are time-independent. If in addition the utility function is separable and $\rho = r$, the value of consumption will be constant while the value of production declines over time, implying that the country will run a large trade surplus in some initial time interval, to be followed by an interval of trade deficit. A resource boom, in the form of an increase in $\theta$, will result in a higher initial trade surplus and a higher steady consumption path. The steady state stock of foreign bonds is also higher.

One might also look at other long-run effects of a resource boom by concentrating on the gradual adjustment of the real wage rate which is institutionally fixed in the short-run. For example, $\tilde{W}$ in Model 3.B may adjust with the state of total unemployment:

$$d\tilde{W}/dt = -\gamma\left(\bar{L}_{MN}-L_N^D-L_M^D\right). \tag{4.7}$$

In this case a resource boom which leads to a <u>short-term fall</u> in E and $Q_N$ (as in Figure 7) actually will cause <u>rise</u> in E and $Q_N$ in the long-run when there is no more wage rigidity.

Finally, one might focus on the scope of factor mobility in the long-run. Take, for example, Model 2.B. In the longer-run, we may want to allow for some capital mobility. Suppose capital in the non-traded goods sector remains immobile but capital is mobile between the two traded-goods sub-sectors.[6] The short-run effects of a boom in Model 2.B are <u>reversed</u> in the long-run in this case, because of supply-side adjustment. Consider Figure 8, where the supply curve $S_N$ for non-traded goods depicts the mar-

---

6) This model is based on Long, N.V. (1981).

ginal cost of production, which is

$$MC = W/MPL_N, \tag{4.8}$$

where W is the wage in terms of the numeraire goods (manufacturing) and where $MPL_N$ is the marginal product of labour in the non-traded goods industry. At any given level of output $Q_N$, the Stolper-Samuelson theorem, applied to the two traded-goods industries, states that a rise in $(P_R/P_M)$ - or equivalently an increase in $\theta$ - will cause W to rise if the resource industry is more labour intensive and to fall if it is more capital intensive (relative to manufacturing).

Consider the case in which manufacturing is more labour intensive. In this case the boom leads to a fall in the $S_N$ curve. This downward shift may result in a new equilibrium with a lower $P_N/P_M$. (If the government pursues a policy of maintaining a constant nominal price for non-traded goods, the fall in $P_N/P_M$ implies a depreciation of the nominal exchange rate. The nominal money supply of course must be increased by credit creation so as to accommodate the rise in nominal income.) In Figure 8, the new equilibrium is at point A, with lower $P_N/P_M$ and higher $Q_N$.

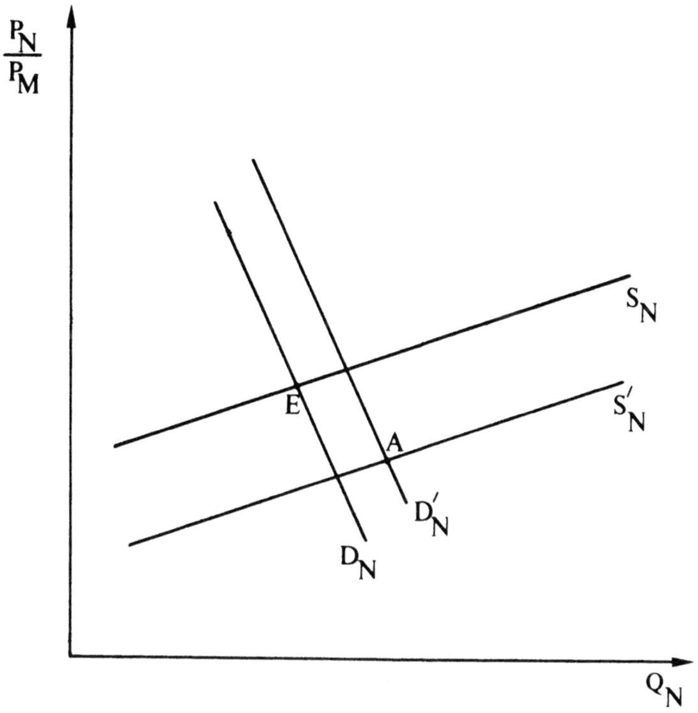


Figure 8

Next, consider the case in which manufacturing is more capital intensive. In this case, the SS curve is shifted upwards, causing $P_N/P_M$ to rise. Two "paradoxical" results may be obtained in this case: the output of manufacturing may rise and the value of output of the resource industry may fall if there is an expansion of non-traded goods output. This is because the increase in $Q_N$ reduces the supply of labour available to the traded-good sector, causing a contraction of output of the labour intensive resource industry, and an expansion of manufacturing. These effects may outweigh the initial tendency which is in the opposite direction if labour is not pulled away from the traded-goods sector.

Similar results can be obtained if we allow capital to move freely between the traded-goods sector and the non-traded goods sector.[7]

So far we have looked at long-run effects from various angles in isolation. Obviously, a more complete analysis would take into account the interdependence between the various long-run adjustments. This is, however, not the purpose of this paper.

## 5. Concluding Remarks

In the present paper we have not attempted a dynamic analysis which links the short-run to the long-run. To the extent that in some cases the long-run effects are the reverses of the short-run effects, the stability of long-run equilibria certainly need careful analysis.

We have also neglected the problem of accumulation of physical capital, which in the real world would inevitably take place in response to disturbances such as an increase in the relative price $P_R/P_M$ or an increase in $\theta$.

7) See Corden, W.M. and Neary, P. (1982).

References:

Corden, W.M. and Neary, P. (1982), "Booming Sector and De-Industrialization in a Small Open Economy", Institute for International Economic Studies, University of Stockholm, Seminar Paper No. 195, February 1982.

Gregory, R.G. (1976), "Some Implications of the Growth of the Mineral Sector", The Australian Journal of Agricultural Economics, Vol. 20, No. 2.

Herberg, H. and Enders, K. (1982), "The Dutch Disease: Causes, Consequences, Cures and Calmatives", Mimeographed, Kiel University.

Hoel, M. (1981), "Employment Effects of an Increased Oil Price in an Economy with Short-Run Labour Immobility", The Scandinavian Journal of Economics.

Long, N.V. (1981), "The Effects of A Booming Export Industry on The Rest of the Economy", mimeo., Australian National University.

Long, N.V. and Sinn, H.-W. (1982), "Surprise Prices Shifts, Taxation Changes, and Supply Behaviour of Resource Extracting Firms", Discussion Paper No. 214-82, University of Mannheim.

Neary, P. and Purvis, D. (1981), "Sectoral Shocks in a Dependent Economy: Long-Run Adjustment and Short-Run Accommodation", Institute for International Economic Studies, Seminar Paper No. 188.

Snape, R.H. (1977), "The Effects of Mineral Development on the Economy", The Australian Journal of Agricultural Economics, Vol. 21, No. 3.

# More on the Consequences of a Resource Boom and the Cures of the Dutch Disease*)

by

Horst Herberg and Klaus Enders

## 1. Introduction

Starting with the pioneering articles by Eide (1973) and Gregory (1976) there has been a quickly growing flow of publications on the consequences of a resource boom on open, raw material producing and exporting economies. Of special interest have been the adverse side-effects of a boom, especially the tendency towards de-industrialisation and temporary unemployment and the need of factor reallocation. As they were first observed (in mo-

---

*) This paper generalizes and extends the analysis of the resource-boom problem and the Dutch disease in Enders-Herberg (1982). Our earlier paper has been discussed in seminars at the University of Oslo, the Norwegian School of Economics and Business Administration in Bergen and the University of Mannheim. As the present study indirectly benefitted much from these discussions we thank again, among others, J. Aarestad, O. Bjerkholt, M. Hoel, E. Hope, the late L. Johansen, L. Lorentsen, A. Sandmo, M. Schmid, H. Siebert and H.-W. Sinn. We are also grateful to the Deutsche Forschungsgemeinschaft for financing a research project under which Enders worked. As usual we accept sole responsibility for any error or deficiency.

We dedicate this paper to Hans Möller who fathered and furthered the research program of which this project is part.

dern times) in the Netherlands following the North Sea gas finds these effects have been taken to be an economic malady, the "Dutch Disease".[1)]

It is well known that highly developed countries will experience a gradual decline in the relative size of their manufacturing sectors. The following table indicates, however, that there have been striking differences over the decade 1970-80: The share of the manufacturing sector in total employment in the Netherlands (NL) has fallen by 23.7 percent, in Norway (N) by 19.5 and in the Federal Republic of Germany (D) merely by 8 percent. This certainly calls for an explanation. The Dutch disease hypothesis claims that these differences are mainly due to the impact of the resource booms in the Netherlands and in Norway.

Share of the Manufacturing Sector in Total Employment (1970 = 100)

| | 1971 | 1972 | 1973 | 1974 | 1975 | 1976 | 1977 | 1978 | 1979 | 1980 |
|---|---|---|---|---|---|---|---|---|---|---|
| NL | 97.7 | 95.3 | 93.3 | 92.7 | 89.7 | 86.0 | 83.0 | 80.0 | 77.7 | 76.3 |
| N | 98.8 | 96.8 | 96.0 | 96.0 | 93.6 | 90.8 | 88.8 | 84.5 | 82.9 | 80.5 |
| D | 99.0 | 97.5 | 97.6 | 96.7 | 94.2 | 93.1 | 93.2 | 92.5 | 92.0 | 92.0 |

Sources: OECD Economic Surveys: Netherlands, April 1981, Table 18, p. 34; Nasjonal Regnskap 1970-1981, Statistik Sentralbyra, Oslo 1982, Table 56, p. 196/7; Sachverständigenrat, Jahresgutachten 1981/82, Table 17, p. 251.

It will be shown that one should distinguish between two pure types of a resource boom, caused either by higher domestic production or higher world market prices of exportable raw materials. The first type we shall call a *resource-output boom* and the second one a *resource-price boom*.

---

1) However, it should not be forgotten that, although a resource boom will have negative side-effects, on balance it improves the overall economic situation of a country experiencing it. This contrasts starkly to the situation of a resource-importing country that faces a resource-price increase and suffers, inter alia, a real income loss. (Cf., e.g., Herberg-Hesse-Schuseil (1982) and the literature cited there.)

Some raw materials require virtually no variable inputs of such domestic factors of production that could also be used elsewhere in the home economy.[2)] If this is the case a resource-output boom simply means higher export receipts and hence amounts to a nominal transfer from the foreign to the domestic economy.[3)] Under the same conditions a resource-price boom is equivalent to a combination of a nominal transfer and a terms-of-trade increase compensated for income changes.

The nominal transfer has an income/spending effect and, as long as trade is not balanced and the home economy through hoarding accumulates wealth, also a wealth/spending effect. Moreover, there is a factor-movement effect associated with the adjustment of the domestic sectors' production to the new demand conditions. Combined these effects result in price, wage, output and employment changes. If raw materials are used domestically as inputs the terms-of-trade increase has a fourth effect, namely a cost effect.[4)] (These effects will be described and studied in more detail below.)

---

2) This seems to be true for,oil and natural gas but not for coal and ores. (In the former case resource revenues are mainly rental income.)

3) Hence the well-known transfer debate, starting with the discussion between Keynes (1929) and Ohlin (1929), has been the forerunner of the present discussion about resource booms and the Dutch Disease. (This fact seems to have gone largely unnoticed.) As the transfer debate in the '20s was evoked by the concern about the feasibility and the economic impact of German reparation payments we are led to conjecture that the problem in question is really an old one. Since the Roman Empire and other once powerful ancient nations extorted huge tribute payments from their enemies and neighbours it could well be that their downfall was partly due to a chronic infection from the malady we now call the Dutch disease (and instead might aptly rename, for such cases, the "conqueror's syndrome").

4) Corden-Neary (1982) introduced the terms "spending effect" and "resource-movement effect". The former one is our income/spending effect, the latter is more general than our factor-movement effect as Corden-Neary also allow for factor re-allocation between resource extraction and other productive activities.

Most papers on the resource-boom problem which follow a general equilibrium approach like those by Corden-Neary (1982), Enders-Herberg (1982), Long (1983), Neary-Purvis (1982), Snape (1977) and Wijnbergen (1982), among others, disregard domestic resource use. The only exceptions known to us are papers by Bruno (1982), Bruno-Sachs (1982a,b), Enders (1982) and, in a short remark, Corden-Neary (1982). The present paper also deals with the more general case.

Our interest is two-fold: Firstly, we want to take another look at the transient and permanent consequences of both types of a resource boom and particularly at the cost effects. It will be shown that the latter can, under exceptional circumstances, lead to pro-industrialization but that they normally strengthen the tendency towards de-industrialization. Secondly, we are interested in an evaluation of various policies advocated or adopted as cures of the Dutch disease. Our main conclusion will be that most policies have favourable results in the shorter run but are ineffective or outright detrimental in the longer run.

The model of a small open economy on which our analysis is based shares basic features with the Scandinavian model, especially the distinction between an exposed sector producing tradeables ("manufactures") and a sheltered sector producing non-tradeables ("services"). Labour and raw materials are the only variable factors, workers are initially immobile between sectors, and the sector that can afford to pay the higher wage rate is the wage leader. Moreover, resource extraction does not require variable labour input. Domestic absorption depends on income and wealth and is spent in fixed proportions on manufactures and services. Finally, we only deal with the case of fixed exchange rates.

Our procedure is as follows: In the next section we outline the model and discuss some of its basic properties. The third and fourth section are devoted, respectively, to the analysis and explanation of the boom effects and the evaluation of six policy alternatives. A short final section contains a few concluding remarks.

## 2. The Model

We study a two-country world with a small domestic economy and a large foreign economy. There are three domestic sectors, a traditional exposed sector producing manufactures, a sheltered sector producing services, and a resource sector producing raw materials. Manufactures are tradeable final commodities, services non-tradeable final commodities, and raw materials tradeable intermediate products.

### 2.1 Notation

M,S,R subscript or superscript referring to manufactures, services, raw materials and to the corresponding sectors

$Q_i$ output of sector i = M,S,R

$L_i, R_i$ input of labour, raw materials in sector i = M,S

$F^i$ production function of sector i = M,S

$\varepsilon^i$ degree of homogeneity of $F^i$

$P_i$ home currency price of commodity i = M,S,R

$P_i^*$ foreign currency price of commodity i = M,R

W nominal wage rate

e exchange rate (home currency price of a foreign currency unit)

A nominal absorption

$Y = P_M Q_M + P_S Q_S + P_R(Q_R - R_M - R_S)$ nominal income (NNP)

$V, V^d$ actual, desired nominal wealth

$D_i$ quantitative domestic demand for commodity i = M,S

$F_L^i := \partial F^i/\partial L_i$, $F_{LL}^i := \partial F_L^i/\partial L_i$ etc.

$\hat{x} := dx/x$ relative change of x

$E(x,y) := (y/x)(\partial x/\partial y)$ partial elasticity of x with respect to y

$a_L^i := E(F^i, L_i)$, $a_R^i := E(F^i, R_i)$ output elasticities

$b_{LL}^i := E(F_L^i, L_i)$, $b_{LR}^i := E(F_L^i, R_i)$, $b_{RL}^i := E(F_R^i, L_i)$,

$b_{RR}^i := E(F_R^i := E(F_R^i, R_i)$

Some additional symbols will be introduced later.

## 2.2 Assumptions

(A 1) Production of raw materials requires no variable factor inputs. The output level is determined exogeneously, for example by the domestic government.[5)]

(A 2) Manufactures and services are produced with labour and raw materials as variable inputs:

$$(1) \qquad Q_i = F^i(L_i, R_i), \quad i = M,S$$

The production function $F^i$ is defined over some non-empty open cone in $R_+^2$ with the origin as vertex, and it is strictly quasi-concave and homogeneous of degree $\varepsilon^i < 1$. Moreover, over the domain of definition,

$$(2) \qquad \begin{array}{llll} F^i > 0, & F_L^i > 0, & F_R^i > 0, & \\ F_{LL}^i < 0, & F_{RR}^i < 0, & F_{LR}^i = F_{RL}^i > 0, & i = M,S \end{array}$$

Productivity changes due to technical progress do not occur. There are also fixed factors of production like capital equipment but they do not depreciate.

---

5) This is basically true, e.g., for oil and gas production on Norwegian fields.

(A 3) Marginal cost pricing of factors and commodities prevails:

$$(3) \qquad P_i F_R^i = P_R, \quad P_i F_L^i = W \quad \text{if} \quad Q_i > 0, \qquad i = M,S$$

(A 4) The exchange rate is fixed, and there are no trade impediments. The foreign currency prices of the two tradeable commodities are exogeneously determined on the world market. Hence,

$$(4) \qquad P_i = eP_i^*, \qquad i = M,R.$$

The home currency price of services adjusts instantaneously, if necessary, as to retain an equilibrium in the domestic services market.

(A 5) Workers react to changing job opportunities only with considerable delay. Hence, after a disturbance, labour is initially a specific factor for both the exposed and the sheltered sector. The nominal wage rate is, however, flexible, and at any moment it is at such a level that at least one of these two sectors employs its total current labour force, i.e.

$$(5) \qquad W = \max\,(P_M F_L^{Mf},\ P_S F_L^{Sf})$$

where $F_L^{if}$ denotes the full-employment marginal productivity of labour in sector i. As time goes by, workers who have lost their jobs in one sector will seek, and find, employment in the other sector.

A similar assumption is well-known from the Scandinavian model: The sector that can afford to pay its workers more will be the wage leader. In our model, however, this role is normally played by the sheltered sector since a resource boom can be expected to raise the price of services but to leave the price of manufactures unaffected. Hence the profitability of the sheltered sector tends to improve and the profitability of the exposed sector tends to deteriorate.

(A 6) Nominal absorption depends on nominal income and actual nominal wealth:

$$(6) \qquad A = Y + \alpha(V-kY) = (1-\alpha k)Y + \alpha V$$

with $\alpha$, k positive and constant and subject to the restriction $\alpha k < 1$.

This is a Dornbusch/Mussa-type of absorption function (cf., e.g., Dornbusch-Mussa (1975): Desired wealth is proportional to income, $V^{a} = kY$, and any gap between actual and desired wealth is gradually closed by hoarding, $Y-A = \alpha(V^{d}-V) = \alpha(kY-V)$.

(A 7) A fixed share of total nominal absorption is spent on each of the two final commodities,

$$(7) \qquad P_iD_i = \mu_iA, \qquad i = M,S$$

with $\mu_M$, $\mu_S$ positive and constant and $\mu_M + \mu_S = 1$.

(A 8) The domestic country is a net exporter of raw materials, i.e.

$$(8) \qquad Q_R - R_M - R_S > 0.$$

(A 9) Financial wealth consists of domestic money and some interest-bearing asset(s). Monetary authorities at home and/or abroad keep the interest rate(s) fixed.

It is worth noting that a resource boom due to higher production $Q_R$ has an *income/spending effect*, a *wealth/spending effect* and a *labour-movement effect*. First of all, it raises income and spending and thus causes changes in the price and output of services, the wage rate, manufacturing production and desired wealth. Moreover, since the current account improves there is also a gradual increase in actual wealth that leads to a further rise in spending and hence additional changes in $P_S$, $W$, $Q_S$ and $Q_M$. Finally, workers who have lost their former jobs, normally in the exposed sector, move into the other sector until in the end everybody has found employment. In case of a boom due to a higher price $P_R$ there is also a *cost effect* that directly influences the price of services and indirectly all other domestic variables.

Although they operate more or less simultaneously it is expedient to study these effects, especially the first three of them separately. This is most easily done by distinguishing three kinds of general equilibria. They are defined as follows: A *short-run equilibrium* is characterised by an equilibrium in the domestic market for services, i.e. $D_S = Q_S$. A *medium-run equilibrium* prevails if, in addition, actual wealth equals desired wealth and hence all income is spent on commodities. And a *long-run equilibrium* is reached if there is also full employment in both the exposed and the sheltered sector.[6)]

A complete analysis would, of course, require a careful study of existence and stability properties. Instead we take a short-cut and assume:

(A 10) These three equilibria always exist, are unique and at least locally stable.[7)]

---

6) In economics, the terms short run, medium run and long run are used in a widely varying sense. To avoid confusion and misunderstandings, the definition given here should be kept in mind when reading this paper.

7) Inter alia, this assumption requires that the marginal productivities of the two variable factors have a sufficiently large range of variation as to allow eqs. (3) always to be satisfied.

To have a firm starting point we also suppose that initially the home economy is in a long-run equilibrium. This situation is disturbed by a resource boom, i.e. by a sudden and unexpected rise in the domestic production or the foreign currency price of the raw materials. The home economy then moves through a series of short-run equilibria first towards a medium-run equilibrium which itself is usually transient only, and finally it settles in a new long-run equilibrium.

Below we shall derive, using comparative statics, which changes will occur in the short, the medium and the long run. To prepare the ground for this analysis we have to list the relationships determining the various equilibria. Eqs. (1), (6), (7) and $D_S = Q_S$ can easily be condensed into

$$(9) \qquad (1-\delta)P_S F^S(L_S,R_S) - \delta P_M F^M(L_M,R_M) - \delta P_R(Q_R-R_M-R_S) - \alpha\mu_S V = 0$$

with

$$(10) \qquad \delta := (1-\alpha k)\mu_S.$$

Obviously, a *short-run equilibrium* is described by the five conditions (3) and (9) subject to (4) and (10) and to the additional restrictions (5) and

$$(11) \qquad L_i \leq \bar{L}_i = \text{initial labour input in sector } i = M,S.$$

Basically the same relationships also apply otherwise. For a *medium-run equilibrium* we only have to replace (9) and (10) by

$$(9') \qquad (1-\delta)P_S F^S(L_S,R_S) - \delta P_M F^M(L_M,R_M) - \delta P_R(Q_R-R_M-R_S) = 0$$

with

$$(10') \qquad \delta := \mu_S$$

since then Y = A holds, and for a *long-run equilibrium* we have, moreover, to replace (11) by

$$(11') \quad L_M + L_S = \bar{L} = \text{total labour supply}$$

since then the home economy has returned to full employment.

## 2.3 Some Basic Relationships

Let us also derive some more relationships that will prove useful later. The homogeneity property of the production functions implies, for i = M,S and j = L,R,

$$(12) \quad L_i F^i_L + R_i F^i_R = \varepsilon^i F^i, \qquad L_i F^i_{jL} + R_i F^i_{jR} = (\varepsilon^i - 1) F^i_j.$$

Hence, taking the definition of $a^i_j$ and $b^i_{jk}$ and eqs. (3) into account, we find for i = M,S:

$$(13) \quad a^i_L + a^i_R = \varepsilon^i, \qquad b^i_{LL} + b^i_{LR} = b^i_{RL} + b^i_{RR} = \varepsilon^i - 1$$

$$(14) \quad b^i := b^i_{LR} - b^i_{RR} = b^i_{RL} - b^i_{LL} > 0$$

$$(15) \quad P_R R_i = a^i_R P_i Q_i$$

Total differentiation of (3) and (9) with (4) and (15) applied yields the following system of differential equations:

$$(16)\quad \begin{pmatrix} 1 & -1 & b^S_{LR} & 0 & b^S_{LL} & 0 \\ 0 & -1 & 0 & b^M_{LR} & 0 & b^M_{LL} \\ 1 & 0 & b^S_{RR} & 0 & b^S_{RL} & 0 \\ 0 & 0 & 0 & b^M_{RR} & 0 & b^M_{RL} \\ (1-\delta)P_SQ_S & 0 & P_RR_S & 0 & (1-\delta)WL_S & -\delta WL_M \end{pmatrix} \begin{pmatrix} \hat{P}_S \\ \hat{W} \\ \hat{R}_S \\ \hat{R}_M \\ \hat{L}_S \\ \hat{L}_M \end{pmatrix}$$

$$= \begin{pmatrix} 0 & 0 & 0 & 0 \\ 0 & -1 & 0 & 0 \\ 1 & 1 & 0 & 0 \\ 1 & 0 & 0 & 0 \\ \delta C & \delta(C+P_MQ_M) & \delta P_RQ_R & \alpha\mu_S V \end{pmatrix} \begin{pmatrix} \hat{P}_R \\ \hat{e} \\ \hat{Q}_R \\ \hat{V} \end{pmatrix}$$

with

$$(17)\quad C := P_R(Q_R-R_M-R_S) > 0$$

denoting net resource revenues or, equivalently, nominal resource exports.

An exogeneous disturbance can be expected to cause some unemployment either in the exposed sector ($\hat{L}_M < 0$, $\hat{L}_S = 0$) or in the sheltered sector ($\hat{L}_M = 0$, $\hat{L}_S < 0$). In the former case eqs. (16) apply with the fifth column of the matrix on the LHS deleted, and in the latter case eqs. (16) apply with the sixth column deleted. Denote the determinants of the corresponding new 5x5 matrices by $\Delta_M$ and $\Delta_S$, respectively. By simple calculations, using (13) - (15) and taking into account the signs of the elasticities $b^i_{jk}$ as determined by (2),

$$(18)\qquad \Delta_M = (1-\varepsilon^M)b^M[P_R R_S - b^S_{RR}(1-\delta)P_S Q_S] - b^S b^M_{RR}\delta W L_M > 0,$$

$$(19)\qquad \Delta_S = b^S b^M_{RR}[(1-\varepsilon^S)(1-\delta)P_S Q_S + (1-\delta)WL_S + P_R R_S] < 0.$$

Let any of the exogeneous variables on the RHS of (16) change. Careful inspection of (16) shows that by Cramèr's rule we arrive at the same numerator determinant for the consequent change in $L_M$ or $L_S$. Since $\Delta_M$ and $\Delta_S$ are of opposite sign, this implies

$$(20)\qquad \text{sign } (\hat{L}_M/\hat{J})\Big|_{\hat{L}_S=0} = \text{sign } [-(\hat{L}_S/\hat{J})]\Big|_{\hat{L}_M=0} \qquad \text{for } J = P_R, e, Q_R, V.$$

By assumption (A 5), in the short run there can be no increase in sectoral labour input. Hence eq. (20) confirms that indeed we have to deal only with the two cases $\hat{L}_M \leq 0$, $\hat{L}_S = 0$ and $\hat{L}_M = 0$, $\hat{L}_S \leq 0$. They also comprise the exceptional possibility $\hat{L}_M = \hat{L}_S = 0$.

## 3. Consequences of a Resource Boom

Since the two kinds of a boom, a resource-output boom and a resource-price boom, normally have rather different effects it is expedient to deal with them separately.

### 3.1 The Case of a Resource-Output Boom

Cramèr's rule and some simple but tedious calculations, again partly based on (13) - (15), yield:

$$(21)\qquad \hat{L}_M/\hat{Q}_R = (1/\Delta_M)b^S b^M_{RR}\delta P_R Q_R < 0$$

$$(22)\quad \hat{P}_S/\hat{Q}_R = -(1/\Delta_M)(1-\varepsilon^M)b^M b^S_{RR}\delta P_R Q_R > 0$$

$$(23)\quad \hat{R}_S/\hat{Q}_R = (1/\Delta_M)(1-\varepsilon^M)b^M \delta P_R Q_R > 0$$

$$(24)\quad \hat{R}_M/\hat{Q}_R = -(1/\Delta_M)b^S b^M_{RL}\delta P_R Q_R < 0$$

$$(25)\quad \hat{W}/\hat{Q}_R = (1/\Delta_M)(1-\varepsilon^M)b^S b^M \delta P_R Q_R > 0$$

$$(26)\quad (\hat{P}_S-\hat{W})/\hat{Q}_R = -(1/\Delta_M)(1-\varepsilon^M)b^M b^S_{LR}\delta P_R Q_R < 0$$

Eqs. (21) - (24) also imply that $Q_S$ and $P_S Q_S$ increase while $Q_M$ falls. Consequently: In the short run a resource-output boom leads to a higher price and output of services and a higher nominal wage rate. More important, it hurts the traditional exposed sector by forcing it to reduce production and employment, i.e. by causing there some de-industrialization. In other words, the home economy is infected by the Dutch disease.

For the medium run eqs. (21) - (26) apply with $\delta = (1-\alpha k)\mu_S$ replaced by $\delta = \mu_S$. Hence similar results are valid. But we can be more specific: Consider for the moment again the short run. The higher value of services production indicates that spending on services has risen, and this requires higher nominal income. Since, consequently, desired wealth is larger than before the boom the current account must have turned into surplus and actual wealth begins to increase. From (16) we infer that

$$(27)\quad \text{sign } (\hat{J}/\hat{Q}_R) = \text{sign } (\hat{J}/\hat{V}) \quad \text{for } J = L_M, P_S, R_S, R_M, W.$$

This immediately leads to the conclusion: Over time the gradual accumulation of wealth and the accompanying rise in absorption aggravate the impact effects of a resource-output boom and, hence, in the medium run the home economy suffers from an even more severe attack of the Dutch disease than in the short run.

The analysis of the long run requires some additional effort. Because of (11'), then $dL_M + dL_S = 0$, i.e. $\hat{L}_S = -(L_M/L_S)\hat{L}_M$. Hence in (16) we only have to replace the last two columns of the LHS matrix by the difference between the sixth column and $(L_M/L_S)$ times the fifth column. Define $\lambda := L_M/L_S$. The new coefficient matrix is, with $\delta = \mu_S$,

$$(28)\quad \begin{bmatrix} 1 & -1 & b^S_{LR} & 0 & -\lambda b^S_{LL} \\ 0 & -1 & 0 & b^M_{LR} & b^M_{LL} \\ 1 & 0 & b^S_{RR} & 0 & -\lambda b^S_{RL} \\ 0 & 0 & 0 & b^M_{RR} & b^M_{RL} \\ (1-\delta)P_S Q_S & 0 & P_R R_S & 0 & -WL_M \end{bmatrix}$$

and it obviously has the determinant

$$(29)\quad \Delta = \Delta_M - \lambda \Delta_S > 0.$$

Replacing in (16) the former coefficient matrix by the new one we arrive at the following results for the long run, again with $\delta = \mu_S$:

$$(21')\quad \hat{L}_M/\hat{Q}_R = (1/\Delta) b^S b^M_{RR} \delta P_R Q_R < 0$$

$$(22')\quad \hat{P}_S/\hat{Q}_R = -(1/\Delta)[(1-\varepsilon^M) b^M b^S_{RR} + \lambda(1-\varepsilon^S) b^S b^M_{RR}] \delta P_R Q_R > 0$$

$$(23')\quad \hat{R}_S/\hat{Q}_R = (1/\Delta)[(1-\varepsilon^M) b^M - \lambda b^S b^M_{RR}] \delta P_R Q_R > 0$$

$$(24')\quad \hat{R}_M/\hat{Q}_R = -(1/\Delta) b^S b^M_{RL} \delta P_R Q_R < 0$$

$$(25')\quad \hat{W}/\hat{Q}_R = (1/\Delta)(1-\varepsilon^M) b^S b^M \delta P_R Q_R > 0$$

(26') $(\hat{P}_S-\hat{W})/\hat{Q}_R = -(1/\Delta)[(1-\varepsilon^M)b^M b^S_{LR} + \lambda(1-\varepsilon^S)b^S b^M_{RR}]\delta P_R Q_R$

Taking $\Delta > \Delta_M$ into account it is easy to infer from (21') - (26'):

The medium-run boom effects on the exposed sector and on the nominal wage rate are attenuated as workers who have lost their jobs in the exposed sector seek, and find, employment in the sheltered sector. But even if the home economy has finally completely adjusted, without government interference, to the new economic conditions there will be permanent real changes, most important an expansion of the sheltered sector and a contraction of the exposed sector, i.e. some de-industrialisation.

These findings can be easily corroborated: As unemployed workers move into the sheltered sector the upward pressure on wages is weakened and the nominal wage rate declines to some extent from its medium-run peak. This improves the profitability of the exposed sector. Consequently, not only the output of services but also the production of manufactures increase. At the same time nominal income and domestic commodity demand rise. Whether, on balance, there is a tendency for an excess demand or an excess supply of services remains indeterminate. Hence there may be a further increase or some decrease in the price of services.

So far we did not look into changes of *real* income. Let the domestic price level P be a linear homogeneous function of the prices $P_M$ and $P_S$ of the two final commodities with partial elasticities that equal the initial expenditure shares in absorption:

(30) $E(P,P_i) = P_i D_i/A = \mu_i, \quad i = M,S$

Define real income y as Y/P. Confining our attention to the medium and the long run, i.e. to situations with A = Y, we find[8)]

(31) $\hat{y} = (C/Y)\hat{P}_R + (P_R Q_R/Y)\hat{Q}_R + (W/Y)(dL_S + dL_M)$.

The present case is characterized by a rise in resource output at a constant resource price. From (21) we easily infer that in the medium run $P_R Q_R \hat{Q}_R + W\,dL_M > 0$. Moreover, in the long run, $dL_S + dL_M = 0$. Consequently, as was to be expected, a resource-output boom raises real income in the medium run and even more in the long run.[9)]

In our earlier paper Enders-Herberg (1982) we studied the case that domestic production of services and manufactures does not require an input of raw materials. Inspection of (16) shows that $R_i = 0$, i = M,S is equivalent to $b^i_{RR} = -1$, $b^i_{RL} = b^i_{LR} = 0$. Hence eqs. (21) - (26) and (21') - (26') hold with only minor modifications. Especially, for $R_S = 0$ and $R_M \geq 0$:

(32) $\hat{Q}_S/\hat{Q}_R \begin{cases} = 0 \\ > 0 \end{cases}, \quad (\hat{P}_S - \hat{W})/\hat{Q}_R \begin{cases} = 0 & \text{in the short \& medium run} \\ > 0 & \text{in the long run} \end{cases}$

Not surprisingly, aside from these rather obvious changes our conclusions remain valid if the exposed or the sheltered sector or even both produce without raw materials. This confirms our former findings.

---

8) Here we made use of eqs. (1) and (3) which imply, for i = M,S, $P_i\,dQ_i - P_R\,dR_i = P_i F^i_L\,dL_i + P_i F^i_R\,dR_i - P_R\,dR_i = W\,dL_i$.

9) With respect to the short run we recall that domestic production and consumption of services increase. Moreover, more is spent on manufactures, and as their price remains unchanged, domestic consumption of manufactures also reaches a higher level. This clearly indicates that an output boom raises real income in the short run as well.

All results derived so far can easily be explained and corroborated by simple economic reasoning (cf. ENDERS-HERBERG (1982)). Details are left to the reader. We only add two observations:

(i) In the medium run the home economy is subject to more forceful influences than in the short run since the wealth/spending effect buttresses the income/spending effect.

(ii) The labour-movement effect counteracts the wealth/spending effect. Hence the initial changes are larger (smaller) than the permanent ones whenever the former effect is stronger (weaker) than the latter.

## 3.2 The Case of a Resource-Price Boom

Let us now analyse the implications of a resource-price boom ($\hat{P}_R > 0$). Following such a disturbance the price of services is not only affected by changing demand conditions but also, as already mentioned, by changing cost conditions. The latter deserve special attention. The basic question is whether or not a higher price of raw materials, via its *cost effect* alone, induces an increase or a decrease in $P_S$. A special and exceptional situation arises if there is an increase and even by a larger percentage than the rise in spending on commodities. Since then the quantity of services demanded declines it is the sheltered and not the exposed sector that has to reduce production and most likely also employment. (That this can indeed happen will be shown later.)

To isolate the cost effect we have to concentrate on the price relationship (3). Suppose that $P_M, W, L_M, L_S$ remain constant and that $P_R$ changes. Total differentiation of (3), taking the definition of the $b^i_{jk}$ and (13) and (14) into account, yields:

$$(33)\quad \begin{bmatrix} 1 & b^S_{RR} & -b^M_{RR} \\ 0 & -b^S & 0 \\ 0 & 0 & -b^M \end{bmatrix} \begin{bmatrix} \hat{P}_S \\ \hat{R}_S \\ \hat{R}_M \end{bmatrix} = \begin{bmatrix} 0 \\ \hat{P}_R \\ \hat{P}_R \end{bmatrix}$$

Therefore,

$$(34)\quad \hat{P}_S/\hat{P}_R = B/b^S b^M$$

with

$$(35)\quad B := b^M b^S_{RR} - b^S b^M_{RR} = b^M_{LR} b^S_{RR} - b^S_{LR} b^M_{RR}.$$

Hence the cost effect of a higher resource price raises (lowers) the price of services if B is positive (negative).

From the pure theory of international trade we know that the reaction of the commodity price ratio to a change in the factor price ratio is closely related to the intersectoral factor-intensity differential. A similar relationship can be expected to hold here as well. Denote the raw material intensity $R_i/L_i$, $i = M,S$, by $\rho_i$. Making use of $F^i_{LR} = F^i_{RL}$ and of eqs. (3) and (13), we find:

$$b^i_{LR} = R_i F^i_{LR}/F^i_L = \rho_i L_i F^i_{RL}/F^i_L = (P_R/W)\rho_i b^i_{RL}$$

$$(36)\quad \text{sign } B = \text{sign } [(b^M_{LR}/b^M_{RR}) - (b^S_{LR}/b^S_{RR})]$$

$$= \text{sign } [\rho_M (b^M_{RL}/b^M_{RR}) - \rho_S (b^S_{RL}/b^S_{RR})]$$

$$= \text{sign } [\rho_S - \rho_M + (1-\varepsilon^S)(\rho_S/b^S_{RR}) - (1-\varepsilon^M)(\rho_M/b^M_{RR})]$$

Thus, not surprisingly, for linear homogeneous production functions ($\varepsilon^M = \varepsilon^S = 1$) a well-known result reappears: The cost effect of an increase in the raw material price raises (lowers) the price of services if they are produced relatively raw-material intensive (labour intensive). Under decreasing returns this price relationship is slightly more complicated but, of course, the intersectoral raw-material intensities still matter.

It seems to be more likely that the production of services is more labour intensive than the production of manufactures, and to such an extent that B and thus the cost effect just discussed are negative. (If services require no resource input at all we have $B < 0$ for $R_M > 0$ and $B = 0$ for $R_M = 0$.)

We have now prepared the ground to deal with our main problem. By similar calculations as before, again based on (16) and (13) - (15), we find:

$$(37) \qquad \hat{L}_M/\hat{P}_R = (1/\Delta_M)[B(1-\delta)P_SQ_S + b^S b^M_{RR}\delta C - b^M P_R R_S]$$

Thus $\hat{L}_M/\hat{P}_R < 0$ if the value of B does not exceed a certain positive margin, especially if it is negative. For reasons just explained it can be expected that $L_M$ will indeed decline. We shall call this the *normal case*. It prevails, for example, if the sheltered sector produces with no or only a relatively small input of raw materials. The following relationships then also hold:

$$(38) \qquad \hat{P}_S/\hat{P}_R = (1/\Delta_M)[B\delta WL_M + (1-\varepsilon^M)b^M(P_RR_S - b^S_{RR}\delta C)] < 1$$

$$(39) \qquad \hat{R}_S/\hat{P}_R = -(b^M/\Delta_M)\{\delta WL_M + (1-\varepsilon^M)[(1-\delta)P_SQ_S - \delta C]\} < 0$$

$$(40) \qquad \hat{R}_M/\hat{P}_R = -(1/\Delta_M)\{b^S\delta WL_M + b^S b^M_{RL}[(1-\delta)P_SQ_S - \delta C]$$

$$- b^M[P_RR_S - b^S_{RR}(1-\delta)P_SQ_S]\} < \hat{L}_M/\hat{P}_R < 0$$

(41) $\hat{Q}_i/\hat{P}_R < 0, \quad i = M,S$

(42) $$\hat{W}/\hat{P}_R = -(1/\Delta_M)\{b^S b^M_{LR}\delta WL_M + (1-\varepsilon^M)b^M[b^S_{LR}(1-\delta)P_SQ_S - b^S\delta C + P_RR_S]\} < 1$$

Note that $P_S$ and W may change into either direction but that the factor-price ratio $W/P_R$ must decline. A fall in $P_S$ and, a fortiori, in $P_SQ_S$ occurs if the cost effect is negative and strong enough to outweigh the positive income/spending effect.

Evidently, the medium-run changes are described by the last equations with $\delta = \mu_S$. Moreover, then from (31)

(43) $$\hat{y}/\hat{P}_R = (1/Y\Delta_M)\{(1-\varepsilon^M)b^M C[P_RR_S - b^S_{RR}(1-\delta)P_SQ_S] + WL_M[B(1-\delta)P_SQ_S - b^M P_RR_S]\}.$$

The sign of $\hat{y}/\hat{P}_R$ is generally indeterminate.

We arrive at the following conclusions: Normally, especially if the sheltered sector needs little or no raw materials, a resource-price boom will lead in the short and the medium run to some unemployment in the traditional exposed sector, to less domestic use of raw materials, and to lower production of both final goods. Hence the home economy suffers from a more severe attack of the Dutch disease than under a resource-output boom. It cannot be ruled out that the value of the output of the sheltered sector shrinks. This would be a particularly pernicious situation as it is associated with a decrease in nominal income. If this happens, i.e. if initially the current account has turned into deficit and hence actual wealth decreases, then the decline in the production of manufactures will gradually be reduced but the decline in the production of services aggravated. An increase in income and wealth, however, brings about a further fall in manufacturing output and a smaller fall in services output. Moreover, it is even possible that in the short and the medium run real income decreases.

For the long run we have to return to eqs. (16) with the new coefficient matrix (28) and again $\delta = \mu_S$. Some simple though tedious calculations yield:

$$(37')\quad \hat{L}_M/\hat{P}_R = (1/\Delta)[B(1-\delta)P_SQ_S + b^Sb^M_{RR}\delta C - b^MP_RR_S] < 0$$

$$(38')\quad \hat{P}_S/\hat{P}_R = (1/\Delta)[BWL_M + (1-\varepsilon^M)b^M(P_RR_S - b^S_{RR}\delta C)]$$
$$+(\lambda/\Delta)\{[B + (1-\varepsilon^S)b^M]P_RR_S - (1-\varepsilon^S)b^Sb^M_{RR}\delta C\} < 1$$

$$(39')\quad \hat{R}_S/\hat{P}_R = -(b^M/\Delta)\{WL_M + (1-\varepsilon^M)[(1-\delta)P_SQ_S - \delta C]\}$$
$$-(\lambda/\Delta)\{[B + (1-\varepsilon^S)b^M](1-\delta)P_SQ_S + b^Sb^M_{RR}\delta C\} < \hat{L}_S/\hat{P}_R$$

$$(40')\quad \hat{R}_M/\hat{P}_R = -(1/\Delta)\{b^SWL_M + b^Sb^M_{RL}[(1-\delta)P_SQ_S - \delta C]$$
$$- b^M[P_RR_S - b^S_{RR}(1-\delta)P_SQ_S]\}$$
$$-(\lambda/\Delta)b^S[(1-\varepsilon^S)(1-\delta)P_SQ_S + P_RR_S] < \hat{L}_M/\hat{P}_R < 0$$

$$(41')\quad \hat{Q}_M/\hat{P}_R < 0, \qquad \hat{Q}_S/\hat{P}_R \gtreqless 0$$

$$(42')\quad \hat{W}/\hat{P}_R = -(1/\Delta)\{b^Sb^M_{LR}WL_M$$
$$+ (1-\varepsilon^M)b^M[b^S_{LR}(1-\delta)P_SQ_S - b^S\delta C + P_RR_S]\}$$
$$-(\lambda/\Delta)b^Sb^M_{LR}[(1-\varepsilon^S)(1-\delta)P_SQ_S + P_RR_S] < 1$$

(43') $\hat{y}/\hat{P}_R = C/Y > 0$

In the normal case the long-run effects of a resource-price boom are a redistribution of labour towards the sheltered sector and an increase in real income. Output of manufactures is lower but output of services need not be higher than in the pre-boom situation. Moreover, total domestic resource use may have fallen.

In the special case $R_S = R_M = 0$ and thus $a_R^S = B = 0$ eqs. (21)-(26), (21')-(26'), (37)-(42) and (37')-(42') indicate that both types of a resource boom have the same consequences. (For example, in the short and medium run $L_M$ and $Q_M$ decline, $Q_S$ remains constant, and $P_S$, $P_S Q_S$ and W increase by the same percentage.) This confirms results reported in Enders-Herberg (1982).

As already mentioned it is possible although rather unlikely that with $L_S$ constant $L_M$ would have to rise. This would require that services production is sufficiently more raw-material intensive than manufacturing. In fact, then $L_S$ must fall while $L_M$ remains unchanged. Let us quickly glance at the implications. Some simple but partly tedious calculation based on (13) - (16) yield:

(44) $$\hat{L}_S/\hat{P}_R = (1/\Delta_S)[B(1-\delta)P_S Q_S + b^S b^M_{RR}\delta C - b^M P_R R_S] < 0$$

(45) $$\hat{P}_S/\hat{P}_R = -(1/\Delta_S)\{B[P_R R_S + a_L^S(1-\delta)P_S Q_S] + (1-\varepsilon^S)(b^M P_R R_S - b^S b^M_{RR}\delta C)\} > 0 \text{ as } B > 0$$

(46) $$\hat{R}_S/\hat{P}_R = (1/\Delta_S)\{[B + (1-a_R^S)b^M](1-\delta)P_S Q_S + b^S b^M_{RR}\delta C\} < \hat{L}_S/\hat{P}_R < 0$$

(47) $\hat{R}_M/\hat{P}_R = (b^S/\Delta_S)[(1-a_R^S)(1-\delta)P_SQ_S + P_RR_S] < 0$

(48) $\hat{W}/\hat{P}_R = (1/\Delta_S)b^S b_{LR}^M[(1-\delta)P_SQ_S + \delta P_RR_S] < 0$

(49) $(\hat{P}_S+\hat{Q}_S)/\hat{P}_R = -(1/\Delta_S)\{[B + (1-a_R^S)b^M]\delta P_RR_S + b^S b_{RR}^M \delta C\} > 0$

For the medium run these equations are valid with $\delta = \mu_S$. The sign of $\hat{y}/\hat{P}_R$ is indeterminate. Therefore:

Under exceptional circumstances that require a strong cost effect due to a sufficiently higher raw-material intensity of services than of manufactures, a resource-price boom can lead, initially and over time, to some unemployment in the sheltered sector, to less domestic use of raw materials, to lower production of both final goods and to higher nominal income. The change in real income is indeterminate.

The long-run consequences of a resource boom are described by eqs. (16) with the coefficient matrix (28) independent of whether initially $L_M$ or $L_S$ declines. Hence, eqs. (37') - (43') apply again, except that some of the inequalities no longer hold. In fact, careful inspection shows that

$$\hat{L}_M/\hat{P}_R > 0, \quad 0 < \hat{P}_S/\hat{P}_R < 1, \quad \hat{R}_S/\hat{P}_R < \hat{L}_S/\hat{P}_R < 0, \quad \hat{R}_M/\hat{P}_R < 0,$$

(50)

$$\hat{Q}_S/\hat{P}_R < 0, \quad \hat{Q}_M/\hat{P}_R \gtreqless 0, \quad \hat{W}/\hat{P}_R < 1, \quad \hat{y}/\hat{P}_R > 0.$$

Under exceptional circumstances the long-run effects of a resource-price boom may be a redistribution of labour towards the exposed sector and a decline in the output of services and in domestic resource use. But even then manufacturing production need not increase. In any case the boom raises the permanent level of real income.

So far we inplicitely assumed that if employment in, say, the exposed sector initially declines it will forever remain below its pre-boom level. Let us take a closer look whether this must indeed be the case. Employment changes depend on the sign of $\Theta := B(1-\delta)P_SQ_S + b^Sb^M_{RR}\delta C - b^MP_RR_S$. Remember that in the short run $\delta = (1-\alpha k)\mu_S$ and in the medium and long run $\delta = \mu_S$. Denote the corresponding values of $\Theta$ by $\Theta^s$ and $\Theta^m$, respectively. Obviously both $\Theta^s$ and $\Theta^m$ are negative for $B \leq 0$. On the other hand,

$$(51) \qquad \Theta^s - \Theta^m = (BP_SQ_S - b^Sb^M_{RR}C)\alpha k\mu_S > 0 \text{ for } B > 0.$$

Hence, $\Theta^s \leq 0$ implies $\Theta^m < 0$ while $\Theta^s > 0$ is compatible with $\Theta^m < 0$. This means that if $L_M$ falls in the short run it will never reach again or even exceed its pre-boom level. Not surprisingly, however: If initially a resource-price boom causes lay-offs of service workers the situation may later be reversed with employment in the sheltered sector expanding and in the exposed sector contracting.

For the special case $R_M = R_S = 0$ economic arguments to explain the consequences of a boom have been given in Enders-Herberg (1982). This is a particularly simple situation as then there exist only income/spending, wealth/spending and labour-movement effects. Otherwise, raw material inputs give rise, as we have seen, to an additional cost effect which may either weaken or strengthen the other three effects. It is left to the reader to provide an economic explanation for the various outcomes that are then possible and have been stated above.

Without going into further details we observe that our findings are similar to those of the (few) other authors who also allowed for the possibility that raw materials are needed as domestic inputs; see Corden-Neary (1982), especially p. 25, and the articles by Bruno (1982), Bruno-Sachs (1982a), (1982b) and Enders (1982). For the exceptional case $R_M = R_S = 0$ that is commonly studied our conclusions are again in line albeit partly somewhat more general with those reported in the quickly growing literature on the Dutch disease; cf., e.g., the papers cited in our introduction.

## 4. Policies Against Adverse Boom Effects

Those groups within the home economy that are negatively affected by a resource boom, normally producers and particularly workers in the traditional exposed sector, can be expected to lobby for corrective government actions: The Dutch disease must be cured or at least the suffering relieved. Among the policies that are likely to be strongly advocated, and that indeed have been enacted at times in countries like Norway, are (i) higher government spending on manufactures, (ii) a wage freeze, (iii) a devaluation of the home currency, (iv) subsidization of domestic resource use, (v) subsidization of the traditional exposed sector, and (vi) (higher) tariffs on imports of manufactures. Clearly the effects of these and other similar therapies should be carefully examined and evaluated. In this section we try to make some contributions to such an analysis. We confine our attention to the more likely case that a resource boom leads to some fall in employment in the exposed sector.[10] It will turn out that these policies should either not be adopted at all

---

[10] Hence there is room for some increase in employment in the exposed sector that will be among the short-run and medium-run consequences of some of the policies.

or enacted only temporarily and gradually phased out again. (The same general conclusion has been reached in Enders-Herberg (1982).)

It will be noted that the various results derived below can be explained by simple economic reasoning. But to save space we refrain from offering more than a few basic observations. Instead we refer the reader to our earlier paper.

## 4.1 Demand Policy

If producers and workers in the exposed sector mistake the decline in the output of manufactures as being due to deficient demand they will sooner or later urge the government to buy more of their products. Such a policy is, however, either completely ineffective or at best only mildly beneficial and may in some respects even be harmful. To substantiate this assertion no calculations are needed. Suppose first that the additional government spending on manufactures, $G_M$, is financed by borrowing at home. Total nominal domestic absorption increases by $G_M$, hoarding and thus the current account decline by the same amount to $Y - A - G_M$. Under the prevailing conditions concerning commodity and factor price it does not pay to expand domestic production of manufactures. The additional supply needed comes from abroad, i.e. the import value goes up by $G_M$. Moreover, private wealth accumulation remains the same,

$$(52) \qquad \dot{V} = \underbrace{P_R Q_R - P_M(D_M - Q_M) - G_M}_{\text{trade balance}} \quad \underbrace{+ \; G_M}_{\text{budget deficit}},$$

merely the sources of additional assets partly change. Net capital exports decrease by $G_M$ but this is exactly matched by the domestic government's extra supply of money and bonds. The home economy even risks to lose foreign reserves.

This could at least temporarily be avoided by borrowing abroad part or all of the funds needed. But both modes of financing lead to the same worsening of the domestic net foreign position and also have the same real effects, namely none.[11)]

In case the government finances additional purchases of manufactures by raising income taxes the exposed sector does indeed benefit but via a rather indirect line of causation. Private absorption and private spending on both final commodities decline. Hence the upward pressures from the boom on the price of services and on the nominal wage rate are alleviated and the deterioration of the exposed sector's cost situation is mitigated. Therefore, the fall in its output and employment is reduced.

### 4.2 Wage Policy

Producers and perhaps also the laid-off workers in the exposed sector might well perceive the wage rise as a fundamental source of their difficulties. They then are likely to press for a wage freeze.

We have seen earlier that an output boom and a price boom have quite different effects on the nominal wage rate when it is flexible. Hence we can safely conjecture that the consequences of a wage freeze and the merits of such a policy also depend on the kind of a boom that the home economy experiences. Our subsequent analysis will support this view.

To determine the implications of a wage freeze requires some effort. To simplify matters we assume that when resource reve-

---

11) In both cases the longer term effects can be dangerous or even disastrous as the recent difficulties of resource-rich countries like Algeria, Mexico and Nigeria in servicing their foreign debt and the consequent drastic deterioration of their international credit rating indicate.

nues start rising the nominal wage rate is at once frozen at its pre-boom level. Because of the increase in demand for services the sheltered sector would be willing to hire more workers but at least in the short run and the medium run is unable to do so. Hence in this sector the wage rate falls short of the value of the marginal labour product, and the price relationship $P_S F_L^S = W$ no langer holds. Consequently, in (16) the first equation and, moreover, the second and fifth column which are associated with $\hat{W}$ and $\hat{L}_S$ have to be deleted. The resulting smaller system of differential equations describes the effects of a boom under a wage freeze. By comparing the new results with the former ones we also can infer the influence of a wage freeze on the effects of a boom.

The determinant of the modified coefficient matrix is

(53) $$\Delta_W = (1-\varepsilon^M)b^M[P_R R_S - b_{RR}^S(1-\delta)P_S Q_S] > 0.$$

Let us first study an *output boom*. Then, by Cramèr's rule:

(54) $$\hat{L}_M/\hat{Q}_R = \hat{R}_M/\hat{Q}_R = 0$$

(55) $$\hat{P}_S/\hat{Q}_R = -(1/\Delta_W)(1-\varepsilon^M)b^M b_{RR}^S \delta P_R Q_R > 0$$

(56) $$\hat{R}_S/\hat{Q}_R = (1/\Delta_W)(1-\varepsilon^M)b^M \delta P_R Q_R > 0$$

Denote partial elasticities like $\hat{P}_S/\hat{Q}_R$ etc. by the subscript "fl" if the wage rate is flexible and by the subscript "fr" if the wage rate is frozen. Since clearly $\Delta_M > \Delta_W$, (22), (23), (55) and (56) imply

(57) $$\hat{J}/\hat{Q}_R\Big|_{fr} > \hat{J}/\hat{Q}_R\Big|_{fl} > 0 \quad \text{for } J = P_S, R_S, Q_S, P_S Q_S$$

$$(58)\quad \hat{J}/\hat{Q}_R\Big|_{fl} < \hat{J}/\hat{Q}_R\Big|_{fr} = 0 \quad \text{for } J = R_M, Q_M.$$

Relationships (54) - (58) hold for the medium run with $\delta = \mu_S$. As full employment is always maintained there is no need (and no incentive) for intersectoral labour movements. The medium-run changes are also the long-run ones. Moreover, we have

$$(59)\quad \hat{y}/\hat{Q}_R = (P_R Q_R/Y)\hat{Q}_R + \mu_S a_L^S \hat{L}_S + \mu_M a_L^M \hat{L}_M$$

and hence, taking (31) and $\hat{L}_S = \hat{L}_M = 0$ into account,

$$(60)\quad \hat{y}/\hat{Q}_R\Big|_{fr} \gtreqqless \hat{y}/\hat{Q}_R\Big|_{fl} > 0 \quad \text{in the } \begin{matrix}\text{medium}\\ \text{long}\end{matrix} \text{ run.}$$

Under a wage freeze a resource-output boom leaves unemployment in both the exposed and the sheltered sector and production of manufactures completely unaffected. Its main consequences are a higher price and output of services and higher nominal and real income. In the medium run these increases are larger than in the short run but the same as in the long run. And, at least up to the medium run, they also exceed those under wage flexibility. Moreover, the permanent increase in real income is the same with or without the wage freeze.[12)]

In case of a *price boom* we derive the following relationships:

$$(61)\quad \hat{L}_M/\hat{P}_R = -(1/\Delta_W) b_{LR}^M [P_R R_S - b_{RR}^S (1-\delta) P_S Q_S] < 0$$

---

12) The last result is rather surprising. It should not be overrated since it is mainly due to our definition of the domestic price level and would not hold under a different definition.

(62) $\hat{R}_M/\hat{P}_R = (1/\Delta_W) b^M_{LL} [P_R R_S - b^S_{RR} (1-\delta) P_S Q_S] < 0$

(63) $\hat{P}_S/\hat{P}_R = (1/\Delta_W) [(1-\varepsilon^M) b^M (P_R R_S - b^S_{RR} \delta C) + b^S_{RR} b^M_{LR} \delta W L_M] < 1$

(64) $\hat{R}_S/\hat{P}_R = -(1/\Delta_W) \{(1-\varepsilon^M) b^M [(1-\delta) P_S Q_S - \delta C] + b^M_{LR} \delta W L_M\} < 0$

We are, of course, only interested in the case that if the domestic government would not interfere with free wage bargaining the nominal wage rate would increase. Taking (13), (14), (18), (35), (42) and (53) into account, we find after some simple but a bit tedious calculations based on (37) - (40) and (61) - (64) that for $\hat{W}/\hat{P}_R > 0$ the following inequalities hold:[13)]

(65) $\hat{J}/\hat{P}_R \Big|_{fl} < \hat{J}/\hat{P}_R \Big|_{fr} \; (<0) \quad$ for $J = L_M, R_M, R_S, Q_M, Q_S$

(66) $(0<) \; \hat{P}_S/\hat{P}_R \Big|_{fl} < \hat{P}_S/\hat{P}_R \Big|_{fr}$

(67) $(\hat{P}_S+\hat{Q}_S)/\hat{P}_R \Big|_{fl} < (\hat{P}_S+\hat{Q}_S)/\hat{P}_R \Big|_{fr}$

The last results are not surprising: The negative effects of a price boom on the cost situation of the exposed and the sheltered sector are smaller with fixed than with rising wages. Hence under a freeze both sectors need not cut back their activities as much as otherwise. This also improves the income situation, leads to higher spending and a stronger upward pressure on the price of services.

---

13) For $\hat{W}/\hat{P}_R < 0$ the unbracketed inequality signs are reversed.

In the medium run (61) - (64) are valid with $\delta = \mu_S$ and (65) - (67) also hold. In addition, (31) and (65) then imply, for $\hat{W}/\hat{P}_R > 0$,

$$(68) \quad \hat{y}/\hat{P}_R \Big|_{fl} < \hat{y}/\hat{P}_R \Big|_{fr} > 0.$$

Consider the long run. The higher resource price has raised the production costs of the exposed sector and forced it to reduce output and employment. But those workers that have been laid off will finally find employment in the sheltered sector. The latter, therefore, can expand production beyond the medium-run level. Nevertheless, in the long run the sheltered sector still has vacancies it cannot fill.[14] Moreover, as the reallocation of labour is not accompanied by wage and cost changes the activities of the exposed sector remain on the medium-run level. Moreover, obviously in the long run, again with $\hat{W}/\hat{P}_R > 0$,

$$(68') \quad \hat{y}/\hat{P}_R \Big|_{fl} > \hat{y}/\hat{P}_R \Big|_{fr} > 0.$$

Let us summarize: Suppose that the resource price rises and that a wage freeze is applied to prevent a wage increase that would otherwise occur. Under these circumstances, the resource boom lowers, initially and over time, employment in the exposed sector and production of both services and manufactures but always by less than with wage flexibility. Moreover, the price of services goes up by more than otherwise. Workers who have lost their manufacturing jobs will finally find employment in the sheltered sector. This reallocation of labour does not affect the exposed sector's activities but allows some expansion of

---

14) Since the freeze prevents the nominal wage rate from rising there will be in the long run excess labour demand - and a mounting pressure to lift it.

services production although not to such an extent that it will reach the same level as with wage flexibility. In addition, a wage freeze has favourable effects on real income in the medium run but detrimental permanent effects.

In the special case of $R_M = R_S = 0$ both kinds of a boom again have the same consequences. Eqs. (54) - (56) and (61) - (64) indicate that then only the price of services and nominal and real income increase while production and employment in the exposed and sheltered sector remain at their pre-boom levels.

These findings can be explained by simple economic reasoning; for the special case see our earlier paper.

It appears justified to conclude that a wage freeze is an expedient although not perfect policy against the *transient* adverse effects of either kind of a resource boom, especially as it reduces or even prevents unemployment. It has, however, also negative consequences, namely a higher upward pressure on the price of services. But if the freeze is sustained for too long it impaires a reallocation of labour according to the new optimal pattern of domestic production and specialization and, therefore, prevents the home economy from reaping the full *long-run* benefits of the resource boom. (But the last possibility need not be taken too seriously since producers of services who want to attract more workers by offering higher wages and trade unions that are eager to return to free bargaining will before long demand that the wage freeze is lifted.)

## 4.3 Devaluation

Observing a post-boom increase in imports of foreign manufactures and facing a decline in its own production and profitability the domestic exposed sector is likely to favour a devaluation of the home currency to curtail these imports and to boost domestic production of manufactures.

First of all, a devaluation raises the home currency price of both traded commodities, raw materials and manufactures. Thus, on the one hand, it causes an additional (mild) price boom and, on the other hand, it improves the cost situation of the exposed sector and its national and international competitiveness.

Perusing eqs. (16) once again we find:

$$(69) \quad \hat{P}_S/\hat{e} = (1/\Delta_M)\{(1-\varepsilon^M)b^M[R_R R_S - b^S_{RR}\delta(P_M Q_M + C)] - b^S b^M_{RR}\delta W L_M\} > 0$$

$$(70) \quad (\hat{P}_S+\hat{Q}_S)/\hat{e} = (\delta/\Delta_M)\{(1-\varepsilon^M)b^M[a^S_R Y - b^S_{RR}(P_M Q_M + C)] - b^S b^M_{RR} W L_M\} > 0$$

$$(71) \quad \text{sign } \hat{L}_M/\hat{e} = \text{sign } \hat{R}_M/\hat{e} = \text{sign } (-\hat{R}_S/\hat{e}) = \text{sign } (\hat{P}_S-\hat{W})/\hat{e} = \text{sign } [(1-\delta)P_S Q_S - \delta(P_M Q_M + C)]$$

These equations apply, with the usual changes, to the short and the medium run. Moreover, (71) also holds for the long run. From conditions (9) and (9') for an equilibrium on the services marked we infer that $(1-\delta)P_S Q_S-\delta(P_M Q_M+C)$ is positive in the short run and equals zero in the medium and long run.

In our special case $R_M = R_S = 0$ the same conclusions apply except there is no initial increase in services production.

A devaluation of the home currency would only temporarily alleviate the adverse consequences of a resource boom. If it is large enough it will, for the short run, bring the exposed sector back to full employment but produce some unemployment in the sheltered sector. Once the current account is balanced again, i.e. in the medium run and beyond, it has, however, only nominal but no real effects since it then has raised all prices and the nominal wage rate by the same percentage.

Let us make an additional remark: It is to be feared that when a devaluation did not work as intended the argument could be put forward that it had not been large enough and that the exchange rate should be further increased. Obviously, such a move would bring only temporary relief but add to the already existing inflationary pressures.

## 4.4 Resource-Price Subsidy

Since the adverse consequences of a resource-price boom are partly due to an increase in production costs domestic producers will be interested in receiving raw materials at a lower than the world market price.

Suppose the domestic government agrees to charge at home the pre-boom resource price. Firms in the exposed and the sheltered sector then can base their pricing and production decisions on the old level of $P_R$ (cf. especially eqs. (3)). Therefore, the $\hat{P}_R$-column on the RHS of (16) now equals $\begin{bmatrix} 0 \\ 0 \\ 0 \\ 0 \\ \delta C \end{bmatrix}$. Evidently, the results of a price boom combined with such a subsidy are described by the RHS of (21) - (26) and (21') - (26') with $P_R Q_R$ replaced by $C = P_R(Q_R - R_M - R_S)$. Not surprisingly they are similar to those of an output boom.

The impact of the subsidy is shown by the differences in the $\hat{J}/\hat{P}_R$ without and with the subsidy, i.e. by the C-free terms on the RHS of (37) - (43) and (37') - (43'). Thus we arrive at the following conclusions:[15)]

A resource-price subsidy always raises production and resource use in the sheltered sector and the nominal wage rate. For not too large intersectoral differences in cost effects[16)] it also lowers the price of services and increases employment in the exposed sector. Manufacturing output is likely to be expanded.[17)] Moreover, real income is raised in the medium run but left unaffected in the long run.

Thus such a subsidy also appears to be a sensible policy to lessen the transient negative effects of a price boom by lowering frictional losses but over time it should be gradually reduced to zero since otherwise the domestic economy would be prevented from adjusting to the new world market prices, i.e. the new terms of trade, and thus again be prevented from reaping the full long-run benefits of the international division of labour.

## 4.5 Production-Cost Subsidy

The exposed sector could also lobby for a production-cost subsidy to lower its costs. Suppose the domestic government is

---

15) Although our arguments are based on a special subsidy level the conclusions are obviously more generally valid.

16) These differences are, as we know, represented by B. The highest admissible value of B is determined by $B(1-\delta)P_SQ_S - b^MP_RR_S \leq 0$ and its lowest admissible value by $B\delta WL_M + (1-\varepsilon^M)b^MP_RR_S \geq 0$ in the short and medium run and by $B(WL_M + \lambda P_RR_S) + [(1-\varepsilon^M)+\lambda(1-\varepsilon^S)]P_RR_S \geq 0$ in the long run.

17) A sufficient condition is a not too large input coefficient $R_S/Q_S$ in addition to the restrictions mentioned in the last note.

indeed willing to pay a certain subsidy $\sigma P_M$ per unit of manufacturing output and finance it out of lump-sum taxes. The pricing equations then are

$$(3') \quad P_S F_L^S = (1+\sigma) P_M F_L^M = W, \quad P_S F_R^S = (1+\sigma) P_M F_R^M = P_R.$$

Nominal income remains the same, i.e. $Y = P_M Q_M + P_S Q_S + C$, as the increase in the value of manufacturing production, $\sigma P_M Q_M$, is just matched by the lump-sum tax to finance it.

Assuming that before the boom no subsidy was paid ($\sigma = 0$) total differentation of (3') and (9) yields eqs. (16) supplemented on the RHS by the column $\begin{bmatrix} 0 \\ -d\sigma \\ 0 \\ -d\sigma \\ 0 \end{bmatrix}$. By Cramèr's rule we find for the short and medium run with $\delta = (1-\alpha k)\mu_S$ or $\delta = \mu_S$, respectively:

$$(72) \quad \hat{L}_M/d\sigma = (1/\Delta_M) b^M [P_R R_S - b_{RR}^S (1-\delta) P_S Q_S] > 0$$

$$(73) \quad \hat{P}_S/d\sigma = -(1/\Delta_M) b^M b_{RR}^S \delta W L_M > 0$$

$$(74) \quad \hat{R}_S/d\sigma = (1/\Delta_M) b^M \delta W L_M > 0$$

$$(75) \quad \hat{R}_M/d\sigma = \hat{L}_M/d\sigma + (1/\Delta_M) b^S \delta W L_M > 0$$

$$(76) \quad \hat{Q}_i/d\sigma > 0, \quad i = S,M$$

Furthermore, taking $\hat{P} = \mu_S \hat{P}_S + \mu_M (\hat{P}_M + d\sigma)$ into account, the medium-run change in real income can be seen to be

$$(77) \quad \hat{y} = (W/Y)(dL_M + dL_S) - \mu_M d\sigma = (WL_M/Y)\hat{L}_M - \mu_M d\sigma.$$

$\hat{y}$ is subject to a positive employment effect and a negative price level effect. The sign of $\hat{y}$ is generally indeterminate.

And the long-run changes are as follows:

$$(72') \quad \hat{L}_M/d\sigma = (1/\Delta)b^M[P_R R_S - b^S_{RR}(1-\delta)P_S Q_S] > 0$$

$$(73') \quad \hat{P}_S/d\sigma = (1/\Delta)b^M[\lambda b^S_{RL} P_R R_S - b^S_{RR} WL_M] > 0$$

$$(74') \quad \hat{R}_S/d\sigma = (1/\Delta)b^M[WL_M - \lambda b^S_{RL}(1-\delta)P_S Q_S]$$

$$(75') \quad \hat{R}_M/d\sigma = \hat{L}_M/d\sigma$$

$$+ (1/\Delta)b^S[WL_M + \lambda P_R R_S + \lambda(1-\varepsilon^S)(1-\delta)P_S Q_S]\} > 0$$

$$(76')^{18)} \quad \hat{Q}_S/d\sigma = (1/\Delta)b^M \lambda(1-\delta)P_S Q_S(a^S_L b^S_{RR} - a^S_R b^S_{RL}) < 0$$

$$(77') \quad \hat{y}/d\sigma = -\mu_M < 0$$

Therefore: In the short and medium run a production-cost subsidy raises production of both final commodities, domestic resource use, employment in the exposed sector and the price of services. The medium-run change in real income is indeterminate. In the long run similar changes occur except that the output of services as well as real income decline.

Thus we are led to a similar conclusion as in the previous case: A production-cost subsidy would be a useful measure to avoid or lower frictional losses but to avert long-term real income losses it should be gradually phased out again. However,

---

18) To derive this relationship one has to take into account that $\hat{L}_S = -\lambda\hat{L}_M$, $\hat{Q}_S = a^S_R\hat{R}_S + a^S_L\hat{L}_S$, $WL_S = a^S_L P_S Q_S$, $P_R R_S = a^S_R P_S Q_S$.

the general public and the government might take a different view. Since immediately after the boom $P_SQ_S$ and hence Y rise there is an accumulation of wealth which, as we know, has similar effects as an output boom. Consequently, the initial increase in $L_M$ is later somewhat reduced. A subsidy just large enough to offset the boom-induced short-run decline in employment in the exposed sector would prove to be too small to reach the same objective in the medium run. Thus it must be feared that the domestic government gradually raises the subsidy instead of reducing it.

## 4.6 Import Tariffs

It would be surprising if the exposed sector would not advocate import tariffs as a suitable measure to reduce imports of manufactures and to improve its profitability.[19)]

Suppose the domestic government decided, immediately after recourse revenues started to rise, to levy a duty of $\tau P_M$ per unit on manufactures coming from abroad and to transfer the tariff proceeds back to the public. The pricing equations are the same as in the previous case (see(3')) with $\sigma$ replaced by $\tau$. Nominal disposable income, $Y^d$, consists of two components, total factor income including resource revenues, $Y^f = (1+\tau)P_MQ_M+P_SQ_S+C$, and tariff proceeds, $Y^t = \tau P_M(D_M-Q_M)$:

$$(78) \qquad Y^d = Y^f + Y^t = P_MQ_M + P_SQ_S + C + \tau P_MD_M$$

---

19) It will be recalled that in the pre-boom equilibrium and in all later medium-run and long-run equilibria trade is balanced and hence manufactures are imported. We assume that this is the case in short-run equilibria as well.

Assume that nominal absorption, A, depends on disposable income as described by eq. (6) and that it is spent according to eq. (7).[20] Then, in the short run,

$$A = (1-\alpha k)[P_M Q_M + P_S Q_S + C + \frac{\tau}{1+\tau}(1+\tau)P_M D_M] + \alpha V$$

and hence

$$(79) \qquad A = \eta(1-\alpha k)(P_M Q_M + P_S Q_S + C) + \eta\alpha V$$

where

$$(80) \qquad \eta := [1 - \frac{\tau}{1+\tau}(1-\alpha k)\mu_M]^{-1}$$

Therefore, the equilibrium condition for the domestic services market is

$$(81) \qquad (1-\eta\delta)P_S Q_S - \eta\delta P_M Q_M - \eta\delta C - \eta\alpha\mu_S V = 0$$

with, as before $\delta = (1-\alpha k)\mu_S$.

Suppose that initially the tariff rate had been zero. Under these circumstances the RHS of (16) has to be amended by $\begin{pmatrix} 0 \\ -d\tau \\ 0 \\ -d\tau \\ Td\tau \end{pmatrix}$

with

$$(82) \qquad T := [\delta(P_M Q_M + P_S Q_S + C) + \alpha\mu_S V]d\eta/d\tau$$

$$= [\ldots](1-\alpha k)\mu_M > 0$$

---

20) It is easy to check that trade is balanced whenever the services market is in equilibrium and all disposable income is absorbed.

We also note that for the medium and long run we have to redefine

$$(83) \qquad \delta = \mu_S, \quad \eta = [1 - \frac{\tau}{1+\tau}\mu_M]^{-1}, \quad T = \mu_M\mu_S(P_MQ_M+P_SQ_S+C).$$

Hence an import tariff is equivalent to a specific combination of a production-cost subsidy and a resource-output boom.[21) ] A quick inspection of our former findings indicates that some of the more interesting consequences seem to be directionally indeterminate. Therefore, we should look more closely. The effects of a tariff can be found by replacing $\delta P_RQ_R$ by T in (21) - (24) and (21') - (24') and adding the resulting RHS to those of the corresponding eqs. (72) - (75) and (72') - (75'). Then the following relationships emerge in the short and medium run:

$$(84) \qquad \hat{L}_M/d\tau = (1/\Delta_M)\{b^M[P_RR_S - b^S_{RR}((1-\delta)P_SQ_S - T)] - BT\}$$

$$(85) \qquad \hat{P}_S/d\tau > 0$$

$$(86) \qquad \hat{R}_S/d\tau \quad 0$$

$$(87) \qquad \hat{R}_M/d\tau = \hat{L}_M/d\tau + (1/\Delta_M)b^S[\delta WL_M + (1-\varepsilon^M)T] > \hat{L}_M/d\tau$$

in the long run:

$$(84') \qquad \hat{L}_M/d\tau = (1/\Delta)\{b^M[P_RR_S - b^S_{RR}((1-\delta)P_SQ_S - T)] - BT\}$$

$$(85') \qquad \hat{P}_S/d\tau > 0$$

---

21) This is nothing but a well-known result in disguise. One only has to recall that in the present model a resource-output boom basically means an income transfer from abroad.

$$(86') \quad \hat{R}_S/d\tau = (1/\Delta)\{b^M[WL_M + (1-\varepsilon^M)T - \lambda b^S_{RL}(1-\delta)P_SQ_S] - \lambda b^S b^M_{RR}T\}$$

$$(87') \quad \hat{R}_M/d\tau = \hat{L}_M/d\tau + (1/\Delta)b^S[WL_M + (1-\varepsilon^M)T + \lambda P_R R_S + \lambda(1-\varepsilon^S)(1-\delta)P_SQ_S] > \hat{L}_M/d\tau$$

The term $(1-\delta)P_SQ_S - T$ is clearly of some importance. Taking into account that initially $\tau = 0$, i.e. $\eta = 1$ simple transformations yield for the short run

$$(1-\delta)P_SQ_S - T = (1-\delta)\mu_S A - T = \alpha k\mu_S[(1-\alpha k)(P_MQ_M+P_SQ_S+C) + \alpha V] > 0,$$

and for the medium and long run

$$(1-\delta)P_SQ_S - T = \mu_M\mu_S Y^d - T = 0.$$

Thus we can rewrite (84') and (86') as

$$(84") \quad \hat{L}_M/d\tau = (1/\Delta)[b^M P_R R_S - BT]$$

$$(86") \quad \hat{R}_S/d\tau = (1/\Delta)\{b^M[WL_M + (1-\varepsilon^M)T + \lambda(1-\varepsilon^S)T] + \lambda BT\}$$

and, moreover,

$$(87')^{22)} \quad \hat{Q}_S/d\tau = (T/\Delta)\{b^M a^S_R[(1-\varepsilon^M) + \lambda(1-\varepsilon^S)] + \lambda\varepsilon^S B\}$$

---

22) Cf. again note 18.

Defining real income as real factor income, $y^f = Y^f/P$, we find

$$(88) \quad \hat{y}^f = (W/Y)(dL_M + dL_S)$$

Therefore: An import tariff always raises the price of services and normally[23)] also output and employment in the exposed sector. More services will be produced at least in the short and medium run. In addition, the effect on real income is positive in the medium run and nil in the long run.[24)]

Our evaluation of the advantages and disadvantages of a production subsidy applies to an import tariff as well.

The special case $R_M = R_S = 0$ now deserves some attention. Taking $b^i_{RL} = b^i_{LR} = 0$, $b^i_{RR} = -1$, $i = M,S$ and $B = 0$ into account we see that in the short and medium run $P_S, Q_S, L_M$ and $Q_M$ rise following the introduction of an import tariff and, more interestingly, in the long run

$$(89) \quad \hat{L}_i/d\tau = \hat{Q}_i/d\tau = 0, \quad i = M,S$$

and

$$(90) \quad \hat{P}_S/d\tau = 1, \quad \text{i.e. } P_S/(1+\tau)P_M = \text{const.}$$

---

23) A sufficient condition for this "normal" outcome is $B < b^M P_R R_S/T$, especially $B \leq 0$.

24) The fact that both outputs $Q_S$ and $Q_M$ can rise seems, at first sight, to contradict the conclusion that real income does not change. But the increase in $Q_S$ and $Q_M$ is matched by the higher domestic resource use and the consequent fall in resource revenues (which are part of factor income).

Hence, an import tariff has no permanent real effects on the home economy if the resources are not used as an input for domestic production.

The basic reason for this result is that the import tariff leaves the terms-of-trade, $P_R/P_M$, and, in the long run also the domestic commodity price ratio $P_S/(1+\tau)P_M$ unchanged.

## 5. Extensions and General Conclusions

In Enders-Herberg (1982) we also argued that the results derived from our former, more restrictive model are more generally valid. For example they hold with only minor modifications if

a) the wage rates paid by the sheltered and the exposed sector differ but always move into the same direction,
b) following a boom the resource sector raises the wage rate for its own workers and thereby sets the pace for wage increases elsewhere in the home economy,
c) the expenditure shares of the two final commodities are not constant but change with relative prices,
d) the marginal rate of absorption is higher for resource revenues than for other kinds of income,
e) all sectors use capital as another factor of production.

The reader can easily convince himself that our former line of reasoning applies to the present model as well and that, therefore, the findings derived in this paper are again more universally valid.

Therefore, we feel entitled to draw the following general conclusions with regard to the fixed exchange rate case:[25)]

---

25) Similar conclusions can be expected to apply to the flexible exchange rate case as well. Then a resource boom adversely

*(i) A resource boom will have favourable overall but adverse sectoral effects on a country experiencing it. Normally the sheltered sector will benefit from the boom while the exposed sector, i.e. the traditional exporting and import-competing industries, will face a decline in its international competitiveness and be forced to reduce its output and employment. Only if the boom is due to a resource price increase and if the sheltered sector is highly resource intensive opposite changes may occur. In any case low labour mobility will initially lead to some unemployment and to overshooting phenomena with respect to the activity level of the shrinking sector.*
*(ii) Government policies to fight the negative side-effects of a boom have negative side-effects themselves. On balance the policies discussed above, i.e. demand or wage policies, resource-price or production-cost subsidies, devaluation, import-tariffs, are either outright detrimental or have desirable consequences only during the adjustment period to a full-employment situation. If enacted at all they should gradually be phased out again as otherwise they tend to prevent the country from reaching its new optimal production and trading pattern.*

As already mentioned one should distinguish between transient and permanent effects of a boom. The permanent adverse effects on some industries could be considered as the price the country has to pay for the permanent beneficial overall effects. Transient adverse effects are a different matter: They should be minimized. In the present context they can be due to (i) low labour mobility combined with some form of wage leadership, (ii) a short-lived boom or (iii) a lasting boom with large erratic changes in resource revenues. Suitable policies to reduce them obviously would be measures to improve labour mobility

---

affects the international competitiveness of the country's exposed sector by causing a revaluation of its currency. (This view is supported, for example, by findings of Neary-Purvis (1982).)

in the first case and investing part of the resource revenues abroad in the second and third case.[26)]

A final remark seems to be called for: Our relationships can also be used to study the consequences of a *resource bust,* i.e. a decline in resource revenues. Thus they describe, for example, the changes a country has to undergo when a boom comes to an end. Moreover, for $C < 0$ they apply to the case of an economy that is a *net importer* of raw materials and faces a rise in their price. Hence they shed some light on the phenomenon of imported inflation-cum-recession in resource-poor countries.[27)]

---

26) It has to be doubted, however, that governments will resist the temptation or the public pressure to spend increasing resource revenues. And they tend be hesitant or unable to cut back costly programmes if revenues fall. Thus, an investment policy, although it is sometimes a reasonable policy, faces severe obstacles. For a more detailed discussion cf. Norman (1982).

27) On this problem see also, e.g., Herberg (1981) and Herberg-Hesse-Schuseil (1982) and the references given there.

References:

Bruno, M. (1982), Adjustment and Structural Change under Supply Shocks, Scandinavian Journal of Economics, Vol. 84, pp. 199-221.

Bruno, M. (1982a), Sachs, J., Energy and Resource Allocation: A Dynamic Model of the "Dutch Disease", Review of Economic Studies, Vol. 49, pp. 845-859.

Bruno, M. (1982b), Sachs, J., Input Price Shocks and the Slowdown in Economic Growth: The Case of U.K. Manufacturing, Review of Economic Studies, Vol. 49, pp. 679-705.

Corden, W.M., Neary, P. (1982), Booming Sector and De-Industrialization in a Small Open Economy, Economic Journal, Vol. 92, pp. 825-848.

Eide, E. (1973), Virkninger av Statens Oljeinntekter på Norsk Økonomi, Sosialøkonomen No. 10, pp. 12-21 (see also University of Oslo, Institute of Economics Reprint Series No. 106.

Enders, K. (1982), Die "Holländische Krankheit" oder Probleme eines sektoralen Booms, Universität Kiel, mimeo. (rev. version: The Dutch Disease or Problems of a Sectoral Boom, Diskussionsbeiträge aus dem Institut für Theoretische Volkswirtschaftslehre der Universität Kiel, No. 47, 1983).

Enders, K. (1982), Herberg, H., The Dutch Disease: Causes, Consequences, Cures and Calmatives, Diskussionsbeiträge aus dem Institut für Theoretische Volkswirtschaftslehre der Universität Kiel, No. 45 (to be published in Weltwirtschaftliches Archiv, September 1983).

Gregory, R.G. (1982), Some Implications of the Growth of the Mineral Sector, Australian Journal of Agricultural Economics, Vol. 20, pp. 71-91.

Herberg, H. (1981), Importierte Zwischenprodukte und monetäre Außenhandelstheorie, in: G. Bombach, B. Gahlen, A.E. Ott (eds.), Zur Theorie und Politik internationaler Wirtschaftsbeziehungen, Tübingen (Mohr-Siebeck), pp. 215-264.

Herberg, H. (1982), Hesse, H., Schuseil, A., Imports of Intermediate Goods and the Efficiency of Fiscal Policy under Flexible Exchange Rates, Weltwirtschaftliches Archiv, Vol.118, pp. 104-130.

Keynes, J.M. (1929), The German Transfer Problem, Economic Journal, Vol. 39, pp. 1-7.

Long, N.V. (1983), On the Short-Run and Long-Run Effects of a Resource Boom, this volume.

Neary, J.P. (1982), Purvis, D.D., Sectoral Shocks in a Dependent Economy: Long-Run Adjustment and Short-run Accomodation, Scandinavian Journal of Economics, Vol.84, pp. 229-253.

Norman, V. (1982), Risk Management in Norwegian Petroleum Policy, in: Petroleum Risks - Economic Risk Aspects of Norwegian Oil Activity, Proceedings of the Bergen Conference on Oil and Economics, Bergen, May 1982, pp. 2-10.

Ohlin, B. (1929), The Reparation Problem: A Discussion, Economic Journal, Vol. 39, pp. 172-178.

Snape, R. (1977), Effects of Mineral Development on the Economy, Australian Journal of Agricultural Economics, Vol. 21, pp. 147-156.

Wijnbergen, S. van (1982), Inflation, Employment and the Dutch Disease in Oil Exporting Countries: A Short-Run Risequilibrium Analysis, World Bank, Washington, D.C., mimeo.

# Taxation of the Australian Resource Sector

by

Michael G. Porter*

## 1. Some Institutional Background

The sharp hike in world energy prices in 1973 and the further rise in 1979, raised the prospect of considerable economic expansion in the Australian mining sector with particular strength in coal, gas and the bauxite/aluminium industry. While these improved trading conditions foreshadowed sizable increases in Australia's national income, a number of factors have combined to create a feeling in parts of the community that such mineral sector expansion would be of little overall benefit and would be capable of harming some groups. It has been argued, for example, that the mineral sector is exceptionally profitable yet pays little tax. It is also argued that mineral exports appreciate the currency, in real terms, and thereby make it more difficult for import-competing firms and other exporters to survive, with a resultant loss of employment and profitability. A sector seen by some as offering somewhat marginal benefits to the community is obviously, in their eyes, a candidate for special taxation burdens, and there has been considerable pressure from such groups for additional taxation of the mining sector.

---

* Professor Porter is Director, Centre of Policy Studies, Monash University. The suggestions of Dr. D. Nellor are gratefully acknowledged, and parts of this paper contain information set out fully in Nellor (1982).

Table 1.1 shows that the product of the mineral industry more than doubled in the ten years between 1966-67 and 1976-77. Moreover, the industry's trend rate of growth is more than twice. that of gross domestic product and exceeds that of any other industrial category. Thus the mineral industry is of primary importance for Australia's economic growth.[1]

While the industry's growth brings it to public attention, and has encouraged the view that it can be taxed with little consequence, experience suggests that its development can easily be stifled. To indicate the industry's responsiveness to price signals, Tables 1.2 and 1.3 present some recent data on exploration for petroleum. Clearly exploration activity is extremely sensitive to economic conditions. For example, private exploration expenditure increased by 250 per cent between 1976 and 1979, following import parity pricing for oil. If taxes dampen those price signals the level of activity could fall just as dramatically, since Australia might then become less attractive for investment in exploration. The importance of the oil industry for Australia's economic growth, combined with this sensitivity to price, suggests that mineral tax policy is crucial for Australia's economic development.

---

1) See Centre of Policy Studies, (forthcoming), Interdependence of the Mineral Sector and the Australian Economy.

Table 1.1: Mining and Gross Domestic Product at Constant Prices (1974-75 base year)

| | Percentage Share of Mining in Gross Domestic Product | Index of Gross Domestic Product in Mining | Index of Gross Domestic Product | Percentage Change from Previous Year | |
|---|---|---|---|---|---|
| | | | | Mining | GDP |
| 1966-67 | 2.15 | 384 | 686 | | |
| 1967-68 | 2.22 | 412 | 711 | 7.1 | 3.6 |
| 1968-69 | 2.44 | 496 | 781 | 20.4 | 9.8 |
| 1969-70 | 2.82 | 603 | 821 | 21.6 | 5.2 |
| 1970-71 | 3.25 | 726 | 857 | 20.4 | 4.3 |
| 1971-72 | 3.34 | 769 | 884 | 5.9 | 3.1 |
| 1972-73 | 3.58 | 850 | 912 | 10.5 | 3.2 |
| 1973-74 | 3.57 | 911 | 980 | 7.2 | 7.5 |
| 1974-75 | 3.84 | 1,000 | 1,000 | 9.8 | 2.1 |
| 1975-76 | 3.30 | 880 | 1,022 | -12,0 | 2.2 |
| 1976-77 | 3.57 | 981 | 1,056 | 11.5 | 3.3 |
| 1977-78 | 3.59 | 1,004 | 1,072 | 2.3 | 1.5 |
| 1978-79 | 3.56 | 1,046 | 1,130 | 4.2 | 5.3 |
| Trend rate of growth | - | - | - | 7.9 | 4.0 |

Source: ABS Catalogue No. 5211.0.

Table 1.2: Australian Real Private and Government Expenditure on Petroleum Exploration (a) ($ millions)

| | Private | Subsidy (b) | Govt. (c) | Total | Percentage Change from Previous Year |
|---|---|---|---|---|---|
| 1970 | 123.59 | 16.27 | 6.18 | 146.04 | - 9.41 |
| 1971 | 115.82 | 9.50 | 6.98 | 132.30 | 21.59 |
| 1972 | 144.78 | 9.24 | 6.84 | 160.86 | - 17.56 |
| 1973 | 115.71 | 10.28 | 6.62 | 132.61 | - 16.09 |
| 1974 | 99.74 | 6.21 | 5.33 | 111.28 | - 16.40 |
| 1975 | 57.60 | 2.44 | 4.90 | 64.94 | - 41.64 |
| 1976 | 42.71 | 0.82 | 4.44 | 47.97 | - 26.13 |
| 1977 | 66.76 | 0 | 3.69 | 70.45 | 46.86 |
| 1978 | 81.03 | 0 | 3.56 | 84.59 | 20.07 |
| 1979 | 150.00 | 0 | 3.27 | 153.27 | 81.19 |

(a) Deflated by the Implicit GDP deflator; 1974/75 = 100.
(b) Payments made under the Petroleum Search Subsidy Act (1958) (no longer in existence).
(c) State and Federal (excluding subsidies).

Source: ABS Catalogue No.8407.0

Table 1.3: Petroleum Exploration and Development Activity in Australia (1975-81)

| | 1975 | 1976 | 1977 | 1978 | 1979 | 1980 | 1981 (a) |
|---|---|---|---|---|---|---|---|
| Seismic Exploration (line km) | 7800 | 24200 | 11600 | 44421 | 41539 | 62685 * | 93500 |
| Exploration Wells Drilled | 25 | 19 | 21 | 53 | 52 | 94 | 158 |
| Development Wells Drilled | 4 | 13 | 20 | 39 | 56 | 29 | 80 |

* Figures estimated by Australian Petroleum Exploration Association in the absence of BMR data.

(a) Estimates by BMR.

<u>Source:</u> Bureau of Mineral Resources

Efficient development of the mineral sector depends on decisions which must be made in a constantly changing environment. Decisions about the timing and location of exploration expenditure, opening of new mines, and the scheduling of extraction from particular mines, must be based on the latest information if they are to be successful. Clearly a considerable degree of entrepreneurship - or alertness to new opportunities - is required. While governments are not, for understandable reasons, generally noted for their business acumen, they do have a crucial part to play in establishing a stable and predictable regulatory and taxation environment in which those in the private sector can make effective long term decisions.

Long lead times are characteristic of mining projects. For example, the search for hydrocarbons off the North West Shelf began in 1963, but the gas discovered will not reach the market before the mid 1980s, and only some years after that will the project start to generate profits. Since 1963 we have seen the rise of OPEC, and some would argue that we will see its demise before any North West Shelf gas is piped to Perth. Clearly, the backers of this project have responded to major changes in world energy markets, since these are of fundamental significance for the viability of their investment.

The North West Shelf is an extreme example, but there are few mining projects whose lead times are sufficiently short to exclude the possibility of dramatic changes in market conditions before the project yields returns. Since all the relevant factors cannot be known, investment decisions have to be based on the current imperfect state of knowledge. Clearly, knowledge is a crucial input to business decision making, and the quality of decision making is directly related to the availability of information. If Governments create a stable business environment (in which, for example, taxes do not vary unpredictably), they allow decision-makers to focus on the multitudinous market uncertainties which they must inevitably confront, without the "noise" of arbitrary Government actions which blur market signals.

2. Mineral Profits, Taxation and Riskiness

There is considerable controversy surrounding the level of taxes paid by members of the mining industry in Australia despite the fact that, as a percentage of gross operating surplus, company tax payable in 1977-78, (the most recent figures available) for example, was 29.4 per cent in mining, c.f. 21.6 per cent in manufacturing. Comparable figures in 1967-68 were 14.6 per cent and 22.1 per cent respectiveley, reflecting the extensive taxation deductions associated with capital expenditure on mines in the previous mineral boom. On an aggregate basis then, it is clear that mining is a major contributor to the total tax take.

While it is true that the top 5 per cent of mining companies tend to fare better than the top 5 per cent of all companies, it is also true that the median mining company in the 1970s was less profitable (whether measured by return on shareholders funds or return on total assets) than the rest of the corporate sector (see Charts 1 and 2). It is of the very essence of the mining industry that there be the occasional bonanza accompanied by large numbers of mediocre or unsuccessful mining ventures. Mining is a risky business, and, like other risky businesses, the distribution of profitability has a greater variance than the more predicatable manufacturing and service sectors. For example, in 1979-80 the return on shareholders funds after deducting taxation and interest was 7.2 per cent for the median company in the mining industry, but 11.3 per cent for all companies; whereas the top 5 per cent of mining companies received a return of 82.8 per cent on shareholders funds in comparison to a figure of 28 per cent for all companies.

Clearly a few mining ventures are highly profitable - such profitability is the lure needed to offset the mean expectation of below normal profitability. While horse racing is fun, it takes the prospect of a reasonable prize to induce owners to prepare horses to race. So too in less pleasant activities such as exploration in remote regions, it takes the possibility of sizable profits for companies to accept the risks and burdens inherent in the search for new mineral deposits. Perhaps the most dangerous illusion prevalent in Australia is that it is possible somehow to cream off the above normal profits, often mis-labelled "rents", without significantly reducing mineral sector activity (see the note below on recent Northern Territory proposals). The fundamental flaw in this argument, however, is that prior to sinking a well or drilling a hole it is precisely the prospect of some sort of bonanza which encourages the miners to continue in areas other than those of high mineral prospectivity. Any special taxation on super profits, then, is actually a tax on the marginal mining prospect - and at some time in their lives, all mines are marginal.

Chart 1 Return on Shareholders' Funds
Performance of Top Companies and Median Companies (%)
After Interest and Tax

Chart 2 Return on Total Assets
Performance of Top Companies and Median Companies (%)
Before Interest and Taxes

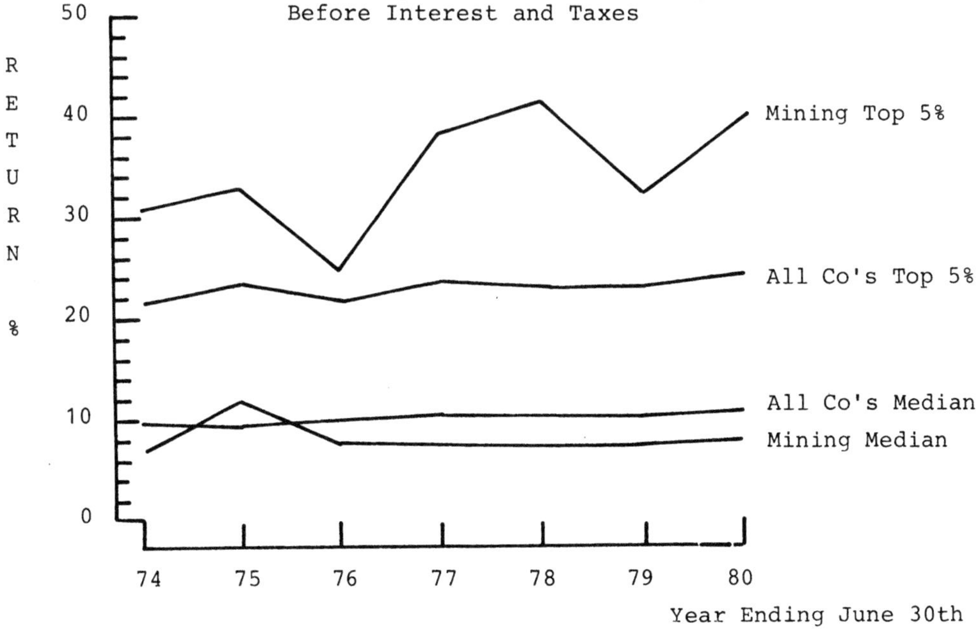


Source: PA Australia Profitability Year Bank 1980.

Chart 1 Return on Shareholders' Funds
Performance of Top Companies and Median Companies (%)
After Interest and Tax

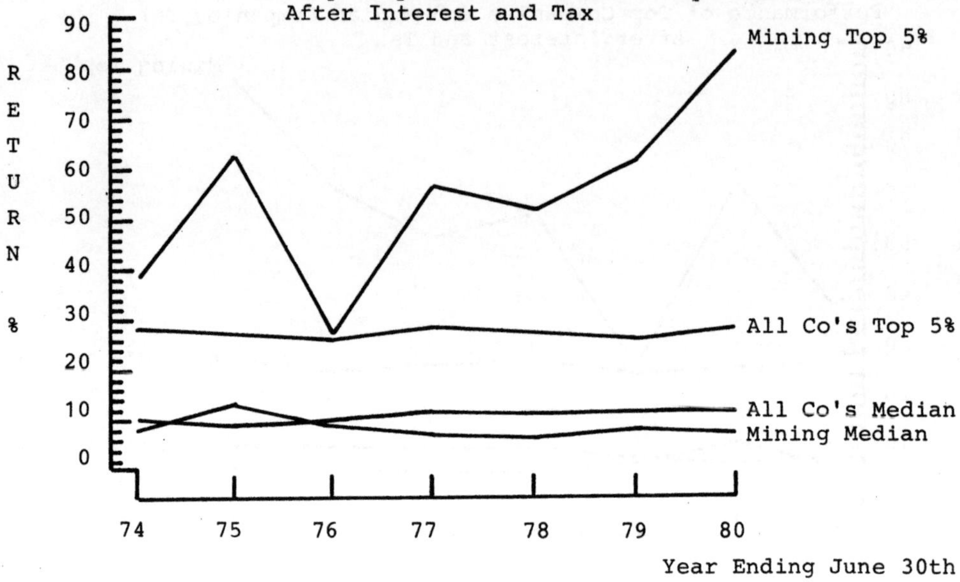


Chart 2 Return on Total Assets
Performance of Top Companies and Median Companies (%)
Before Interest and Taxes

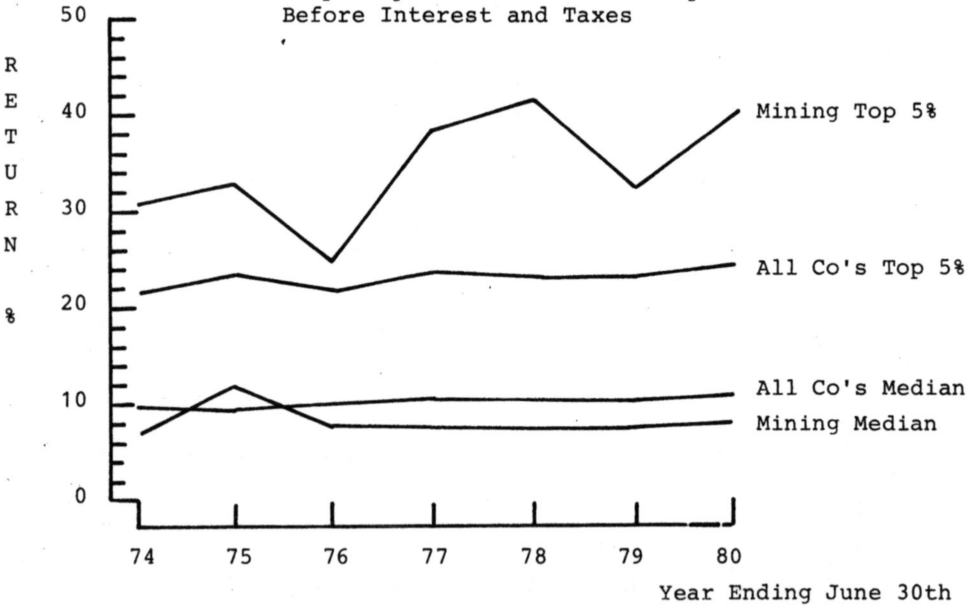


Source: PA Australia Profitability Year Bank 1980.

and to expand the use of capital and labour in sectors offering higher rates of return - e.g. minerals and supporting industries - promises to increase the general level of well-being. So long as labour and capital are encouraged to be mobile - to move in the direction of higher wages and profits - then most of those workers and owners of capital who temporarily lose from the changing relative price structure due to mining expansion should be able to earn higher returns after leaving their prior activity.

Similarly, the derived demand for non-traded goods which expands in the context of mineral expansion generates considerable expansion in the economy generally. Thus while the mineral sector creates upward pressure on the relative price of services and non-traded goods - which are inputs to other sectors, including the protected sectors, and thus may induce some contraction - there is room for considerable optimism over a wide range of industries in association with the expansion of mineral production. (And in Australia, of course, a good deal of the economy may be classified as "non-traded" owing to natural and contrived protection from foreign goods and services.)

In summary, then, while there is a good deal of gloom regarding some implications of mineral sector expansion - our analysis in a variety of studies suggests there is cause for optimism.

## 4. Taxation and the Sale of Mineral Leases

This short note focuses not so much on the industry effects of mineral expansion, but on taxation, and in particular I question the view that there is a case for special taxation arrangements for the mineral sector of the "resource rent tax" variety (see Garnaut and Clunies Ross (1975)). It is argued that so long as mineral leases - in particular those of high prospectivity - are obtained through competitive "arms-length" arrangements, then mineral sector expansion will be based on the acquisition, at market prices, of property rights, in just the same way as the manufacturing sector expansion will be based on the purchase of imputs at market prices. This competitive bidding for leases can take many forms, including bonus bidding and a variety of royalty and/or profit tax arrangements. (In general, royalty bids have the deficiency of tending to reduce mine output, relative to profit based bids, but may involve administrative savings.)

A fundamental point, then, regarding mineral taxation is that in areas of known high prospectivity in Australia - e.g. the Alligator River area, Bass Strait and the Cooper Basin - there should be competitive bidding for mineral leases, with bidding perhaps taking the form of royalty offers, profit sharing arrangements and various combinations, depending on the attitudes of government and participating parties to the sharing of risk. In areas of no known prospectivity the problem of resource "rents" and super profits taxes should not arise and leases would be obtained for essentially nominal "bids", perhaps in exchange for obligations to search. In these cases there is little economic argument in favour of royalty arrangements, since these serve to deter the (full) development of the mine and may actually reduce other tax receipts (e.g. income and indirect taxes). Royalties are a tax on production, and encourage under-utilisation of mineral deposits. For example, if a prospect is utterly marginal (say relative to some investment elsewhere in the economy) why should there be a mineral royalty, when there is no specific output tax in other industries? The effect of a royalty may be premature closure, or failure to start a mine, with a consequent loss of income, taxes and employment.

## 5. The Objectives of Taxation Policy

The ideal tax, from a strict efficiency viewpoint is that which interferes least with maximisation of the present value of income in the community - and this need in no way imply maximising tax revenue - quite the contrary. Equity considerations may lead us to raise a given amount of revenue with least cost, and in this case we wish to maximise output subject to this obligation to meet equity claims and other "needs of government". The proponents of resource rental taxation, on the other hand, often seem to argue that the major - indeed perhaps the only - benefit from mineral sector activity is derived through taxation.[5] However, there is no logical connection between policies capable of maximising tax receipts of government and those maximising the level of well-being in the community. On the contrary, policies which maximise tax receipts in the short-run may simply drive entrepreneurship elsewhere - and in particular, tax policies concerned to maximise the take from the mineral sector may induce resources to go into other sectors, e.g. manufacturing and services which produce lower private and social product. Accordingly, it is crucial to point out that considerations of economic efficiency and equity will always conflict with concerns to maximise the tax take from the mineral sector. If our national product is diminished by failing to expand outputs in industries in which we have a comparative advantage then it will be harder to share the (shrunken) pie with the less well off members of the community.

---

5) For example, Garnaut and Clunies Ross (1975), argue:

> "Industries based on cheap sources of energy or producing fuels and minerals are typically capital-intensive and, in a developing country, they have limited scope for local purchase of supplies. Hence, whatever national benefit is to be derived from them must come mainly through taxation. The central task of economic management in the resource-based industries is thus to maximise the contribution that these industries make to government revenue".

Our concern with efficiency leads us towards preference for taxes which are neutral in their resource allocation effects, since if we could show that decisions by owners of capital and labour were independent of the tax regime, it could then be claimed with some validity that raising of tax revenue on mining offers no threat to the real economic livelihood of the community, nor would it distort the allocation of resources. The difficulty, however, is that there is no such thing as a neutral tax, since by definition a tax is a burden on a particular activity and creates expectations of further burdens in related activities. Even a poll tax (e.g. a tax of $x per head), which is often assumed to be neutral, has real effects in that it encourages people to leave the region in which the poll tax is imposed and go elsewhere. So too special taxation of super profits in the mineral sector will encourage entrepreneurs to look elsewhere.

It is interesting to note in this regard that "super profits" appear to have been earned in the computer and office equipment area in the last couple of years. According to a 1980 survey in Australia (by Personel Administration Pty. Ltd.) the average return on shareholders funds has been 27 per cent over the period 1978-80 in contrast to a figure of less than 8 per cent in the mining sector. Those who would favour special taxation on the basis of super profitability should, then, have been arguing that those in the computer industry be subject to special penalities. Yet it is precisely in these innovative areas that entrepreneurship is currently flourishing, with the prospect of very considerable gains in community wealth, productivity and social income. The notion that we should tax areas of thriving entrepreneurship would seem more dangerous to the general well being than almost all other proposals for intervention.

It could be argued, perhaps, that the difference between the mining sector and, say, the computer industry is that mining involves pure economic rents - "once the well has been developed the oil flows, regardless of taxes" - whereas it takes entrepreneurial and scientific skill to produce a new chip or a profitable application of microelectronic technology. A contrary view is that those individuals who "chose" their partents wisely, or who subsequently were assisted to take useful educational programs, have thereby acquired a highly profitabla endowment of human capital from which they are now earning "quasi-rents", say as designers of chips, or whatever. Accordingly, if there is a case for taxing the "rents" from mineral deposits then there may also a case for taxing all quasi-rents and the rents and educational advantages derived from government handouts. Indeed, if mineral leases were typically auctioned but education were provided free to all takers, then there would be a more powerful case for a special "rent" tax on human capital or "education income" than on mineral output or profits.

In general, then, my suggestion is that so long as all property rights have been obtained through arms-length arrangements, that is so long as I have paid for my education, my mineral lease, or whatever at the going rate, then from there on there is no case for discriminating in the taxation of industries or activities. But if there have been known and valuable handouts of leases (excluding the marginal lease[6] which turns out to be a bonanza) or public funds then special taxation seems a sensible response, on the "user pays" principle.

---

6) A marginal lease is one for which no mining company will pay a significant sum.

## 6. Auctioning of Leases versus Resource Taxation

If there is a case for intervention in the taxation of the mineral sector to achieve efficiency, our arguments suggest that it is most likely to be at the stage at which mineral leases are obtained. Recent evidence of bidding for leases off the U.S. Atlantic coast suggests that the technique is quite workable - even in areas in which technological breakthroughs are required (e.g. offshore drilling at depths of 2000 metres). At present the main use of auction-type techniques in Australia is essentially an "auction-by-work-program" approach, in which companies propose exploration programs, with the company with the largest and most credible exploration program usually proving successful. Such auctions typically lead to an inefficient allocation of resources, since they may encourage excessive exploration and may also arbitrarily redistribute income to those who provide exploration services rather than offering an appropriate return to the community which owns the mineral rights or to the company with exceptional geological insight. Issues related to the increased use of auctions in Australia are canvassed in Robinson (1982).

## 7. Exhaustability and Taxation

A further complication regarding efficiency in mineral taxation is that fear of future taxation may encourage rates of extraction which are well in excess of the preferred rate. This problem is particularly significant with exhaustible resources. Prior to the OPEC action in 1973 oil companies tended to extract rather more oil than was dictated by market conditions, reflecting fear of expropriation by the Arabs. So too, fears of sharp increases in taxes on mineral activities may have the effect of either deterring oil search, for example, or artificially encouraging high rates of extraction prior to the expected imposition of the new impost. It appears clear, then, that if the Australian community is both to obtain a reasonable return on its mineral property rights and to to experience the benefits of an expanded mineral sector, in which Australia has a strong comparative advantage, then there is a real need for agreement on the fundamental principles regarding acquisition of mineral rights. To my mind this implies acceptance of far greater use of market bidding arrangements in areas of high prospectivity. Once the use of auctions is generally adopted, the basis is set for the application of uniform taxation of income across all companies in all industries in Australia.

A particular difficulty regarding expectations, taxation and other imposts, is that there is a very long list of possible ways in which government can extract revenue from, and impose burdens on, mineral projects. For example, in Queensland and other parts of Australia the State governments have imposed rail freights out of all proportion to rail costs, in an effort to extract a larger share of the return from coal mining. Partly as a result of the increasing tendency of governments to devise new means of taxation and expropriation, there is increasing concern by mining companies to negotiate indenture agreements which pin down schedules of charges in relation to provision of water, rail freight, electricity and so forth. One reason the mineral sector in Australia is strongly opposed to competitive auctions, bonus bidding and other "up front" payments, is their belief that there is essentially no limit to the ingenuity of governments in coming up with new forms of taxation. There is a fear that any agreement that auctions were to be the sole means of extracting government share of the rents would subsequently be violated, given the capacity of governments to pass new legislation and overturn old law. Robinson (1982), has analysed some of the issues relating to the interdependence of auction and other tax arrangements, and while indicating a general preference for the use of competitive bidding he makes the basic point that "a well structured negotiation is superior to a poorly designed auction, and a badly structured negotiation is dominated by an appropriate auction". In other words, when it comes to taxation policy in the case of resources, theory does indeed lead us towards preference for auction type arrangements in the case of valuable mineral rights, but consideration of realistic models of government behaviour forces us to accept that auctions may not always be the preferred arrangement.

## 8. Bonanzas

A major difficulty with current debates on mineral taxation is that there are occasional bonanzas which make it seem politically essential that there be some redistribution from the owners of extraordinarily profitable deposits to the community at large. As an example, Bass Strait oil and gas discoveries have been made highly profitable by the rise in the price of oil in recent years, and this has offered extraordinary profits to Esso-BHP and the Gas and Fuel Corporation. Bonanzas have also created academic and political pressure for resource rent taxes.

Some would argue, and I count myself amongst them, that the prospect of bonanza profits is a thoroughly desirable incentive to entrepreneurship, including entrepreneurship in mineral exploration, but also in other areas of scientific and engineering expertise. The possibility of technological breakthroughs which may eventually turn out to be of considerable benefit to mankind is enhanced by the prospect of a bonanza. If we use "super-profits" taxes to knock out the upper tail of the profit distribution then those few who would search out a new mine or technological breakthrough are essentially being signalled to desist, and to join the masses on the middle class road to the middle income. It can rationally be argued that civilisation has progressed largely on the backs of scientific, technical and managerial innovations and other entrepreneurial activities, and that it is simply not worth the potential tax gains from creaming "surplus" off the rich if a major consequence is cessation of significant entrepreneurial activity. Few entrepreneurs are in it for love. Profit signals serve a most useful purpose, as Adam Smith told us two centuries ago, and as economists such as Schumpeter and Giersch have reminded us in the twentieth century.

As an example of the returns to entrepreneurship (and to encouragement of science) the new possibilities offered by satellite techniques and other scientific advances in geology and computing hold forth the prospect of an affluent Australia based to an important degree on expansion of the mineral sector. The fact that a large number of other countries also have highly prospective regions of mineralisation means that any attempt to impose differential taxation in Australia will typically drive mineral activity elsewhere. Just as the bauxite/alumina/aluminium industry expanded in Australia in response to "super-royalties" overseas, so too can such industries depart our shores when so induced by special taxation. Governments may swear that the special taxation of Bass Strait oil or Bougainville copper or other such bonanzas is "one-off", but there is little reason to believe that the massive sums required to undertake mineral exploration, in particular in the oil and gas area, will be forthcoming in Australia if profits taxes of the sort imposed on North Sea oil seem highly probable.

## 9. The Northern Territory - The Proposed Mineral Royalty Bill

It may be helpful to complete this brief note with a reference to recent proposals for special profit-based mineral royalties in the Northern Territory of Australia. While the Northern Territory has some regions of high prospectivity - e.g.

the Alligator River region with its large share of world uranium - the vast bulk of potential mineral projects in the Territory are marginal (and even the more profitable mines are vulnerable, as recent slowdowns at Gove, Groote Eylandt and Tennant Creek have indicated). Analysis of the Territory mineral sector suggests that the recently proposed 35 per cent "profit tax", (with profit being defined by rather special definitions of income and costs)[7], would have had the effect of causing companies to search in areas other than the Northern Territory. Accordingly, while there is some evidence that the Northern Territory may be able to increase tax receipts for one or two years by imposing special taxation arrangements, the bulk of geological evidence regarding the marginal nature of most potential mineral deposits in the Northern Territory suggests that we cannot reject the possibility of a resulting fall-off of mineral activity and thus an eventual reduction in both royalty receipts and the total tax take from mineral activity in the Northern Territory.

## 10. Conclusion

If we introduce competitive bidding techniques for mineral leases, even if they raise little revenue owing to the preponderance of marginal mines of low prospectivity, there will then be no reason for any differential tax treatment of mining income and output. Mining and manufacturing, for example, will be on an equal footing. While depreciation periods should vary, to reflect economic costs which may differ across plant by industry, there is no real case for systematic discrimination against the profits or output of the mining sector.

---

7) See Centre of Policy Studies, 1981.

Finally, we have noted above, that while competitive bidding techniques are our preferred approach to extracting a return from publicly owned mineral rights, there is little confidence in the private sector that acceptance of such auctions will prove to be the sole or last attempt by governments to extract extra revenue. In light of this, greater certainty and increased efficiency of resources may be obtained by properly negotiated indenture agreements which may specify some form of special taxation should the project prove to be a bonanza, and which may also tie governments down, in terms of their capacity to make additional imposts. In other words, we are forced to accept that in designing practical tax law and mineral legislation, the auction is far from being the sole applicable technique - indeed it may prove to be dominated by negotiated arrangements in the form of indenture agreements, legislative and even constitutional constraints.

References:

Centre of Policy Studies, 1981, "An Evaluation of the Northern Territory of Australia Draft Mineral Royalty Bill", Mimeo, October.

L.H. Cook et al., 1982, "The Mining Sector and the Australian Economy", Mimeo, June.

Corden, W.M., 1981, "Exchange Rate Policy and the Resource Boom", Discussion Papers, Centre for Economic Policy Research, Australian National University, March.

Garnaut, R. and A. Clunies Ross, 1979, "The Neutrality of the Resource Rent Tax", Economic Record, Vol.55, No. 150, September.

Gregory, R.G., 1976, "Some Implications of the Growth of the Mineral Sector", Australian Journal of Agriculture Economics, 20, August.

Krueger, A.O. and M.G. Porter, 1981, "The Asset Theory of Exchange-Rate Determination and the Resources Boom", Mimeo, October.

Nellor, D.C.L., 1982, "Taxation of the Australian Resources Sector", Mimeo, September.

Robinson, M.S., 1982, "Oil Lease Auctions: Reconcilling Economic Theory with Practice", Mimeo, November.

# Diversification and Stabilization in a Resource-Exporting Country*

by

Egbert Gerken

## 1. Introduction

The lion's share of foreign exchange is earned by exporting only one or two primary commodities in a group of countries with small and open economies.[1] While some of them find structural adjustment to an appreciating real exchange rate - brought about by the exploitation of newly-found natural resources or by a secular commodity price hike - painful,[2] the "commodity

---

* This paper reports research undertaken in the "Sonderforschungsbereich 86" (Hamburg-Kiel) "Teilprojekt 3" with financial support provided by the "Deutsche Forschungsgemeinschaft". Thanks are due to Hermann Dick and David Vincent.

1) By 1980 a single commodity accounted for at least 40 per cent of total export earnings in 60 member countries of the International Monetary Fund, the commodity being crude petroleum, another mining product or an agricultural product in 22, 15, and 23 countries respectively. In all but two of the reporting countries gross domestic product was smaller than in Switzerland, in all but one of the non-oil exporting countries even smaller than in Finland. The ratio of imports to gross domestic product was higher than .20 in all but eight of the 48 reporting countries.
International Monetary Fund 1982. World Bank 1982.

2) The term commodity is used as short-hand expression for primary commodities. Natural resources are defined as essential and specific factors in the production of commodities. Sectors making use of either exhaustible or inexhaustible natural resources are called mining and agricultural sectors respectively.

problem" of old non-oil exporting countries within the group is rather related to instability of world commodity prices and uncertainty about future price trends.[3] Unless caused by supply shifts of the country in question, fluctuating world commodity prices get transmitted into fluctuating export earnings. These are a major potential source for macroeconomic disturbances in the open economy.

To some extent the market narrows down swings in export earnings by encouraging private adjustment to uncertainty. Only ex-post can a commodity price change be identified as either a deviation from some projected price trend or a trend shift. Thus there is an incentive for investors to diversify their portfolio and for suppliers to enter future contracts. The variance in expected returns is reduced this way and risk is shifted to less risk averse international speculators. A problem will arise, if society considers as inacceptable disturbances - domestic price level changes or employment variations - caused by remaining earnings fluctuations. There will then be excess demand for stability as an economic good. Stabilization, however, is not free of cost.

Security might be among the goods foregone. As will be shown, diversifying investments becomes less rewarding under a

3) Adams and Behrman condense the available information into a few useful indicators. While the fluctuation index for the unit values of manufactured goods increased from 0.0343 in the 1950-69 period to 0.0538 in the 1969-79 period, the index for all primary commodities as a group increased from 0.0479 to 0.1764 between the two periods. The secular real price trend has been negative in the 1950-69 period for all major commodity groups except non-ferrous base metals, but has been positive in the following decade, again with the exception of non-ferrous base metals. The World Bank projects positive real trends up to 1990 for all groups but beverages. These projections, however, are contingent on a multitude of unforeseeable developments. Adams, F.G. and J.R. Behrman 1982, p. 10. World Bank 1980, p. 12.

regime of fixed exchange rates, in particular when foreign exchange reserves or an international compensatory facility are used for financing contra-cyclical policies. As specialization in commodity production increases, the economy is left more vulnerable should a world commodity price decline turn out as permanent. The market, in effect, provides for less security when a specific stabilization policy transfers risk from private economic units to government. In order to regain the good, the authorities might substitute a policy of export diversification - for example taxing commodity exports and subsidizing exports of other goods - for the market solution. The costs of such supplementary measures should then be added to the other costs of the specific stabilization strategy. Export diversification may, however, also be welfare-increasing for reasons other than commodity price uncertainty - serving as first, second or third-best solution to some market imperfection or policy-imposed distortion. The commodity problem would then appear in another light as the severity of earnings fluctuations would be partly due to suboptimal specialization. Removing or compensating for the distortion causing it, excess demand for stability or costs of stabilization policies would also be reduced. If there is a case for export diversification irrespective of the commodity problem, the policy should be applied in any case.

The costs and benefits of export diversification in an old non-oil commodity exporting country are the subject matter of the following analysis. In chapter 2 the causal nexus from commodity price fluctuations to domestic disturbances is developed from well-established macro- and microeconomic theory. As both structural change and multiple distortions are central to the argument, the analysis is promising only in a quantitative multisectoral general equilibrium framework applied to some appropriate country. The case of copper-exporting Chile will be studied here. The country model is described in chapter 3 and documented in the appendix. The model experiments used for determining the costs and benefits are also designed in chapter 3.

The results are presented and discussed in chapter 4 and conclusions are drawn in chapter 5.

## 2. Disturbances in a Small Commodity Exporting Country

Long-run economic equilibrium is characterized by employment at the natural rate and a balanced foreign exchange account. The properties of short-run equilibria in a small commodity exporting country depend on the exchange rate regime. Consider a temporary decline of the leading export commodity price affecting the economy in a state of long-run equilibrium. The public expects inflation to continue at the equilibrium rate. Labour demand in the commodity sector contracts and unemployment increases unless a falling real wage level allows for additional employment in other sectors.

### 2.1 The Case of Flexible Exchange Rates

Without government intervention on the foreign exchange market, a shrinking supply of foreign exchange earned by commodity exporters devalues the domestic currency and raises domestic prices of traded goods accordingly. Labour moves into sectors that respond to rising prices by expanding exports or substituting imports. The domestic credit component of money supply can then be directed at the employment or the price level target. As real income earned in the commodity sector falls, the demand for money is reduced. If opportunity costs of holding money remain unaffected, the domestic price level goes up unless the domestic component of money supply is reduced accordingly. The authorities might then try to exploit money illusion by not fully adjusting domestic credit. As additional inflation would come unexpected, the nominal wage claim would remain unchanged in the short-run. The resulting real wage decline would tend to stabilize aggregate employment in spite of contracting labour demand in the commodity sector.

A free foreign exchange market thus facilitates the stabilization of aggregate employment though at the cost of transmitting export earnings fluctuations to the domestic price level and to sectoral employment. Earnings instability is reduced to some extent by portfolio reactions. As rates of return to capital vary inversely between sectors producing traded goods on the one side and the commodity or non-traded goods on the other side, private investors can reduce the risk of an uncertain commodity price trend by accepting a lower internal rate of return on investment in sectors producing traded goods. The remaining earnings instability, however, still creates economic bads. Price level instability reduces the usefulness of money leading the economy nearer to a system of barter: gains from the specialization of a money economy are lost. Structural employment instability adds to informational frictions in the labour market and thus to a higher natural rate of unemployment.[4]

## 2.2 The Case of Fixed Exchange Rates

Under a fixed exchange rate, a shortfall in earnings drives the foreign exchange account into deficit. Unless outflowing reserves are offset by domestic credit, however, the deficit is automatically eliminated as contracting money supply reduces domestic absorption thereby diminishing import demand and freeing resources for export. Money supply (on account of outflowing reserves) is falling more rapidly than money demand (on account of contracting real income). The price level consequently falls, the real wage level increases and aggregate demand for labour is reduced. If, however, the deficit on current account can somehow be sustained up to a time when the commodity price has recovered, the authorities might attempt to stabilize absorption by expanding domestic credit. This would tend to stabilize the price level and employment as well. The disturbance would in effect be contained within the commodity sector.

4) Phelps, E.S. 1972.

On the other hand, with the variance in returns to capital eliminated in all but the commodity sector, the rewards of portfolio diversification would be much reduced.

The deficit on current account can, perhaps, be financed by international compensatory finance, the depletion of reserves held for precautionary purposes, or by capital inflow. Compensatory finance is available only in limited amounts. Beyond the limit, the reserve stock would have to ebb and flow in order to stabilize absorption under fluctuating export earnings. The average stock must be enlarged and opportunity costs of reserve-holding must be borne.[5] Provided the capital market has been liberalized, capital inflow could be induced by raising the domestic against the foreign nominal interest rate. With the domestic price level nearly constant, such policy would destabilize the real interest rate thus impairing the efficiency of investment allocation.[6] In the following, only the case of reserve-holding is considered. Implicitly, it is always assumed that the capital market is closed.

An activist demand policy is difficult under fixed rates as the authorities must at the same time intervene in the foreign exchange market. If the public believes that the declared policy cannot be maintained, for example on account of insufficient reserves, speculative capital movements will compel the authorities to give up. In defense of the fixed rate, contraction of real domestic absorption would have to be tolerated till the reserve outflow comes to a halt. Deflation then allows for some recovery of demand. Coming unexpected, however, the real wage claim would increase. In short-run equilibrium, therefore, aggregate employment and output supply fall below the natural rate. Labour demand in sectors producing either the commodity or non-traded goods is reduced without an offsetting

---

5) See Tanzi, V. and M.J. Blejer 1982.

6) See Heller, H.R. and M.S. Khan 1978.

expansion in the production of traded goods. In sum: defending the exchange rate against volatile commodity prices but not succeeding in demand management creates costs in terms of aggregate employment fluctuations without stabilizing the domestic price level. The rewards for diversification, furthermore, are smaller than in the case of flexible rates as rates of return to capital do not vary inversely.

## 2.3 Gains and Losses from a Diversification Policy

Export taxes and subsidies can be applied to compensate for lost market incentives to diversify under fixed exchange rates. Besides the intended risk reduction, such measures would also reduce costs of balancing the movements on the foreign exchange account and would mitigate disturbances in case a contracyclical policy fails. There might, however, also be gains and losses irrespective of the commodity problem. If laissez-faire had assured an optimal trade specialization before, the policy would throw away some of the gains from trade. In commodity-exporting developing countries, however, current specialization often is suboptimal for the following reasons:[7]

(1) National monopoly power in commodity trade leads to unequal rates of domestic and foreign rates of transformation in production, unless there is a sole exporter of the commodity, i.e. a private monopolist. An export tax is the first best solution for exploiting the country's monopoly power.

(2) Import protection has been granted to various "infant" industries which never grew up. The resulting overvalued exchange rate hampers production of other traded goods. Export subsidies are a second best solution, dismantling of protection naturally being first best.

(3) Domestic factor markets are distorted, most notably there are static labour cost differentials between rural and urban

---

7) See Corden, W.M. 1974.

regions and between informal and formal sectors.[8] Trade policy can supply a third best solution, while a factor and a production tax-cum-subsidy are first and second best solutions respectively, provided the distortion cannot be removed directly.

If such market imperfections and policy-induced distortions exist and have not been corrected already by other policies, it will not at once be clear whether a specific export tax-cum-subsidy policy will move the economy nearer to the point of optimal specialization or away from it. This can only be determined within a quantitative general equilibrium framework.[9] If the net effect on the variable serving as welfare-indicator turns out as positive, such result will also imply that current export earnings fluctuations are in part originating in market imperfections or policy induced distortions causing suboptimal specialization. Attention should then be directed towards these distortions before turning to stabilization.

## 3. Analytical Framework

In a recent review of economy-wide model building, Powell (1982) classified such models into the Keynes-Klein, the Philipps-Bergström and the Walras-Johansen tradition. These correspond respectively to time-series models built in the Wharton

8) See Gerken, E. 1981.

9) Various aspects of the Chilean commodity problem have already been studied within a quantitative general equilibrium framework: Dick et al (1982) on alternative stabilization targets (employment, absorption, exchange rate), Gerken (1983) on using the exchange rate for stabilizing inflationary expectations, Vincent (1982) on the requirements for monetary policy. The present study makes use of the same model. This allows to focus attention on the benefits and costs of export diversification. For a deeper analysis of the implications of alternative reactions to the instability problem, the reader is referred to the previous studies.

tradition,[10] the continuous time disequilibrium model developed at LSE and the applied general equilibrium school. For the subject at hand a model providing projections as distinct from forecasts is required. Its role is to provide insights into how the economy might be influenced by a particular event in the way of identifying the key factors underlying the projections for endogenous variables. For this reason the model should be tightly constrained by conventional economic theory.

The model used here belongs to the Walras-Johansen class paying close attention to microeconomic theory.[11] As such it is particularly appropriate for an open free market economy, explaining trade flows and the composition of domestic activity by relative prices and substitution prospects. Models of this class centre around an input-output system of accounts which facilitates the inclusion of many types of commodity and factor flows: commodity inputs from domestic and imported sources to current production, to capital creation, to households, government and exports, and industry inputs of primary factors which include different types of labour, fixed capital and a sector-specific factor.

10) For these models, which are formulated in discrete time, relative prices play a minor role by comparison with "activity" variables. For examples see Lasaga (1981) and Adams and Behrman 1982.

11) See Dixon et al. 1982.

The major behavioural postulates are (i) Producers choose their commodity and factor inputs to minimise production costs of a given output subject to three level constant returns to scale industry production functions. At the first level is the Leontief assumption of no substitution between input categories or between them and an aggregate of the primary factors. At the second level are CES functions describing substitution between domestic and imported sources of each input category and between the three primary factors (aggregate labour, fixed capital, natural resources). At the third level are CES functions describing substitution between different occupations within the aggregate labour category. (ii) Households choose their consumption to maximise an additive nested utility function subject to an aggregate budget constraint. The nests of commodity categories contain CES functions describing substitution prospects in consumption between domestic and imported sources of each category.

The comparative-static one period system ignores lags, leads and adjustment dynamics. Hence the model has nothing at all to say about the time path followed by endogenous variables under the influence of an exogenous shock. A short or long-run interpretation can be placed on the adjustment period depending upon the nature of the shock under consideration and the configuration of the economic environment in which it is assumed to take place.

## 3.1 Sector Disaggregation

Trade flows and variations in the rate of return to capital are central to the subject matter of this study. Sector disaggregation must, therefore, emphasize differences with respect to the export share of domestic production, the import share of domestic demand and the cost shares of factors (see Table 1). On the basis of the 67-sector input-output table of Chile in 1977, the economy is disaggregated into eight sectors

Table 1 Structure of Economic Activity, Production Costs and Trade in Chile 1977

| Sector | Sectoral Shares in Total | | | Cost Shares in Domestic Production | | | | | | | Trade Shares | | Relative Wage[7] | Import Protection[8] |
|---|---|---|---|---|---|---|---|---|---|---|---|---|---|---|
| | GDP | Workforce | Exports | Copper | Other Intermediates Domestic | Other Intermediates Imported | Labour | Fixed Capital | Natural Resources | Indirect Taxes, Net | Exports[5] | Imports[6] | | |
| Agriculture | .103 | .079 | .054 | - | .419 | .038 | .115 | .198 | .198 | .032 | .061 | .085 | .631 | .042 |
| Copper Mining | .066 | .065 | .464 | .067 | .290 | .094 | .204 | .171 | .171 | .003 | .836 | .036 | .920 | - |
| Other Mining | .018 | .027 | .055 | - | .341 | .133 | .299 | .125 | .125 | -.023 | .342 | .624 | 1.095 | .050 |
| Food Processing | .081 | .066 | .076 | - | .619 | .096 | .082 | .142 | - | .061 | .058 | .093 | .760 | .036 |
| Light Manufacturing | | | | | | | | | | | | | | |
| - Import Competing[1] | .080 | .090 | .039 | .010 | .490 | .142 | .149 | .154 | - | .055 | .038 | .204 | .894 | .085 |
| - Export Oriented[2] | .018 | .021 | .070 | - | .593 | .055 | .137 | .196 | - | .019 | .294 | .056 | .943 | .094 |
| Heavy Manufacturing[3] | .050 | .063 | .058 | .027 | .484 | .264 | .100 | .071 | - | .054 | .064 | .494 | .952 | .104 |
| Services[4] | .584 | .589 | .184 | - | .323 | .050 | .289 | .282 | - | .056 | .042 | .034 | 1.104 | .001 |

1) Manufacture of consumer good except wood products, cork, and paper. 2) Manufacture of wood products, cork, and paper. 3) All other manufacturing industries. 4) Construction, utilities, distribution, private and public services. 5) Share of exports in total demand for domestic production. 6) Share of imports in total domestic consumption. 7) Ratio of sectoral to economy-wide average wage. 8) Ad valorem rates of import protection.

Source: Presidencia de la República.

each producing one homogeneous good.[12] Natural resource based sectors (agriculture, copper mining, other mining) are distinguished separately. Likewise, a domestic sector characterized by a small export and import share is singled out (services). Activities competing moderately against foreign substitutes (agriculture, food processing) are separated from activities competing strongly, either in the world market (other mining, export oriented light manufacturing) or at home (import competing light manufacturing, heavy manufacturing). Lastly, import competing manufacturing activities are grouped according to different cost shares of imported intermediates.

### 3.2 System of Equations

The model is written as a set of structural equations linear in all growth rates, allowing it to be solved by simple matrix methods. The equations are listed in Table A1, the variables and coefficients are defined in Tables A2 and A3 respectively. Table A1 partitions the equations into five groups:

(1) Final demands. Households, capital creators, government and foreign sources demand both domestic and imported commodities. Substitution between goods of different source is always induced by changes in relative prices of these goods. The extent of substitution, for a given relative price change, is determined by the specific substitution or cross-price elasticity. Households can substitute between domestic and imported sources of their consumption goods (equation (1)). They can also substitute between different commodity categories within their consumption bundles (2). Producers of capital goods can switch their demand between domestic and imported sources of supply (3). Government demands for imported and domestic commodities are related to real consumption expenditure. Finally, equation (5) indicates that provision is made for Chilean exports to influence world commodity prices.

---

12) Presidencia de la República.

(2) Industry Inputs. Chilean industries can substitute between domestic and imported sources of their intermediate inputs, between the primary factors labour, fixed capital, natural resources, and between different labour occupations in producing their outputs (6-9). The extent of substitution for a given change in relative prices is governed by the relevant substitution elasticities.

(3) Zero pure profits. Since constant returns to scale production technology and competitive behaviour is assumed in the derivation of the structural equations, profits can accrue only to factors of production. Industry output prices must equal production costs: intermediate costs from domestic and imported sources, occupational labour costs and fixed capital and land costs (10). The price of a unit of capital creation in each industry must equal its production costs (11). Note that capital creation does involve primary factors indirectly, via their content in intermediate inputs. The selling prices of import commodities must equal the costs of importing (12). Finally, the revenue from exporting must equal the cost of doing so (13).

(4) Market clearing. Supply must equal demand for domestically produced commodities (14), occupational labour (15), fixed capital (16) and natural resources (17). Note that (15)-(17) simply require that factor employment levels are satisfied. Full employment assumptions are not imposed.

(5) Miscellaneous equations. The model includes a large group of equations which are mainly definitional in character. Their structure is for the most part self explanatory. Of these however, equations (22)-(24), which determine the allocation of investment across industries, require further comment.[13] They follow from the assumption that (a) investment takes one period to install,[14] (b) investors have an expected rate of return

13) See also Dixon et al 1982.

14) Since the model is of a one period comparative-static nature, this means that endogenous investment in the model's solution period does not augment the economy's capital stock in that period.

schedule from new investment which is downwards sloping and (c) aggregate investment is allocated across industries to equate expected rates of return.

The monetary equilibrium need not be made explicit in the model. The authorities are assumed to vary domestic credit supply so as to secure the imposed employment, absorption or exchange rate target given changes in money demand and in the foreign component of money supply.

## 3.3 Experiments

The analysis proceeds by a set of comparative-static model experiments. In each experiment, the conditions for a specific equilibrium are imposed via the model closure, i.e. by assigning values to a selection of exogenous variables (see Table A4). From Tables A1 and A2 we see that there are 4gh + 11g + 9h + rh + 2r + 13 equations in 4gh + 15g + 11h + rh + 2r + 17 variables. The model is first closed by assigning values to a selection of 4g + 2h + 4 variables. Solution values for the endogenous variables are then obtained by matrix methods. The solution matrix gives percentage deviations of all endogenous variables from the values which would have occurred without the commodity price change or the diversification policy. In Table 2 a selection of macroeconomic, trade, and sector employment solutions necessary for reaching conclusions is presented.

The first experiment is designed so as to explore the net social costs of an export tax-cum-subsidy policy irrespective of the commodity problem. A 10 per cent ad valorem tax on copper exports and a 10 per cent ad valorem subsidy on the export of all goods but services and products of heavy manufacturing is introduced or added to existing taxes or subsidies. Export quantities of other goods are fixed in all experiments.[15]

15) See footnote 2 to Table A4.

The structural change is expected in the long-run. Labour as well as capital, therefore, move equalizing sectoral factor prices. Real wages adjust so as to allow only natural unemployment. The labour force is kept constant and there is no shift in world copper demand. The solution for real GDP then shows the net real income effect of the diversification policy. Real income is used as the sole welfare indicator, i.e. a positive result for GDP is interpreted as a welfare gain or as indicating negative net social costs of the diversification policy. The sectoral solutions for employment, capital stocks, exports and imports quantify the structural change induced by the policy. These solutions together with the solution for total investment are used to construct the data base for the model describing the economy after structural change has taken place. Each of the following stabilization policy experiments can then be carried through both for the undiversified and for the diversified economy. Comparing solutions, the contribution of the export tax-cum-subsidy can be studied.

All instability experiments have in common the copper price decline and the short-run perspective. A rather drastic copper price shock of -41.37 p.c. is introduced for the following reason. A variation of the reserve stock is considered here as the only means of financing a deficit in current account. In order to secure credibility for their contra-cyclical policy and to prevent speculative capital movements, the authorities must visibly plan the average reserve-stock for the worst expected case. A price decline of the size of the average deviation from the moving five-year-average of the last decade (1970-79) plus two standard deviations has been defined here as the worst expected case.[16] Under normal distribution this would exclude an even more dramatic decline with a probability of 95 per cent. The short-run perspective is characterized by intersectoral capital immobility and by the possibility of unexpected price

16) World Bank 1980, p. 310.

level changes. All short-run model closures exogenously fix sectoral capital stocks and money wage.

The second experiment is designed to bring out the implications of stabilizing aggregate employment under flexible exchange rates. The imposed short-run equilibrium is characterized by a constant balance on current account and by employment at the natural rate. The solutions then show the currency depreciation, the price level increase and sectoral employment changes. The third experiment attempts demand management under fixed exchange rates. The model is now closed by fixing real domestic absorption as well as the nominal exchange rate exogenously allowing the current account to move into deficit. The solutions permit an assessment of the stabilization effects and of the reserve stock required for financing the current account deficit. The opportunity costs of reserve-holding are calculated outside the model. The fourth experiment is intended to study the instability effects under fixed rates without demand management. The model is closed by fixing the balance on current account and the nominal exchange rate.

## 4. Results

### 4.1 Export Diversification

The macroeconomic, trade, and sector employment solutions necessary for reaching conclusions are presented in Table 2. The following interpretation makes extensive use of the cost and trade structure data of the base year collected in Table 1 without at each occasion referring to the Table explicitly.

The first experiment introduces a 10 per cent ad valorem tax on copper exports and a 10 per cent ad valorem subsidy on all other exports except services and products of heavy manufacturing. The experiment allows time for labour and capital to move between sectors, though the specific factor naturally cannot leave agriculture or mining. Copper exports drop by 10.58 per cent in quantity but, owing to Chile's monopoly position, by only 5.24 per cent in foreign currency value. While total export earnings grow by 8.03 per cent following the subsidized expansion of non-copper exports, the share of copper in total exports goes down from 46 to 40 per cent. The real income effect is positive: real GDP is enlarged by 1.43 per cent.

The real income effect must be examined for the underlying distortions, though an exact separation of the general equilibrium result into its elements is not possible. First, observing different export demand elasticities for copper and for all other goods (2 and 20 respectively) as well as infinite supply elasticities for all imports, an appreciation of the Terms of Trade by 1.86 per cent can be calculated from the copper share in total exports (0.46) and the model results for copper and aggregated non-copper export quantities (-10.58 per cent and 20.35 per cent respectively). Weighted by the trade share, the Terms of Trade improvement adds 0.54 per cent to GDP. If no other distortion was included in the model and the data base was describing a country currently exploiting its monopoly power, this outcome would be swamped by the negative income effect of raising marginal copper revenues above marginal costs of supply. Current exploitation must be embodied in the data base as indirect tax or as pure profit in copper production. Since virtually the whole copper output is exported or used as own intermediate, net indirect taxes reduce the domestic price in much the same way as pure export taxes do. The net indirect tax rate on copper output, however, is only 0.003 in the base year. Pure profits, if they existed, would be merged with rental payments to owners of natural resources in the data base. The profit rate, which would be smaller than the earnings share accruing to the sector-specific factor (0.17), must be compared to the optimum export tax rate, which is equal to the reciprocal of the export demand elasticity after imposing the optimum trade

Table 2 Effects of Export Diversification and Alternative Policy Reactions to a Shortfall in World Copper Demand [1]

| Variable | Experiment 1: Export tax-cum-subsidy[5] (long-run closure)[9] | 41.37 per cent world copper price decline (short-run closure)[9] — Experiment 2: Flexible exchange rates and fixed aggregate employment U[7] | D[8] | Experiment 3: Fixed exchange rates and fixed real domestic absorption U | D | Experiment 4: Fixed exchange rates and fixed balance on current account U | D |
|---|---|---|---|---|---|---|---|
| Macroeconomic | | | | | | | |
| Real GDP | 1.43 | -4.50 | -3.53 | -5.71 | -4.67 | -7.56 | -6.00 |
| Real domestic absorption | 1.43 | -4.50 | -3.53 | O(EX) | O(EX) | -7.56 | -6.00 |
| Aggregate employment | O(EX)[6] | O(EX) | O(EX) | -1.17 | -1.33 | -7.18 | -5.56 |
| Exchange rate - nominal | O(EX) | 8.19 | 6.01 | O(EX) | O(EX) | O(EX) | O(EX) |
| - real | -6.74 | 5.02 | 3.53 | 0.28 | 0.33 | 4.50 | 3.37 |
| Domestic price level[2] | 6.74 | 3.17 | 2.47 | -0.28 | -0.33 | -4.50 | -3.37 |
| Wage -nominal | 9.12 | O(EX) | O(EX) | O(EX) | O(EX) | O(EX) | O(EX) |
| - real | 2.43 | -3.17 | -2.47 | 0.28 | 0.33 | 4.50 | 3.37 |
| Trade[3] | | | | | | | |
| Balance of current account | O(EX) | O(EX) | O(EX) | -634 | -562 | O(EX) | O(EX) |
| Aggregate imports | 8.03 | -8.20 | -5.90 | -0.94 | -1.05 | -10.64 | -8.16 |
| Aggregate exports | 8.03 | -8.20 | -5.90 | -20.75 | -17.33 | -10.64 | -8.16 |
| Copper exports | -5.24 | -45.24 | -47.05 | -45.63 | -50.00 | -45.26 | -49.52 |
| Non-copper exports | 19.33 | 23.35 | 29.15 | 0.44 | 4.45 | 18.85 | 19.41 |
| Sector Employment[4] | | | | | | | |
| Agriculture | 1.11 | 4.96 | 3.72 | 0.12 | 0.19 | 0.84 | 0.82 |
| Copper mining | -13.59 | -16.75 | -21.84 | -20.03 | -24.86 | -19.38 | -24.15 |
| Other mining | 8.97 | 21.94 | 16.05 | 0.43 | 0.64 | 6.58 | 5.23 |
| Food processing | 1.04 | 6.39 | 6.63 | 0.15 | 0.26 | -2.31 | 0.12 |
| Light manufacturing | | | | | | | |
| - import competing | 0.39 | 7.98 | 8.58 | 0.84 | 1.02 | -2.44 | 0.49 |
| - export oriented | 16.60 | 21.59 | 16.46 | 0.47 | 0.79 | 8.63 | 7.48 |
| Heavy manufacturing | -6.53 | 6.36 | 4.85 | 2.22 | 1.85 | -2.19 | -1.62 |
| Services | 0.83 | -3.22 | -2.45 | -0.22 | -0.34 | -9.93 | -7.70 |
| Total change in work-places | 2.60 | 5.98 | 5.37 | 1.71 | 1.87 | 8.05 | 6.49 |

1) Model projections. All projections are in percentage changes with the exception of the balance of current account which has the unit of millions of US dollars (1977). 2) Consumer price index. 3) In foreign currency value. 4) For sector disaggregation see footnotes to Table 1. 5) 10 per cent ad valorem tax on exports from copper mining, 10 per cent ad valorem subsidy on exports from all sectors except copper mining, heavy manufacturing and services. 6) Denotes variable exogenously set to zero. 7) Model in base year. 8) Model after updating base year data according to results of experiment 1. 9) The time interpretation of short- and long-run is somewhat vague. In the short-run nominal wage claims and industry capital stocks are fixed, in the long-run they are flexible. The distinction is thus between periods not exceeding the time lag on the adjustment of expectations and the gestation lag on new investment and periods exceeding both lags.

Source: Own Calculations.

tax structure.[17] Though the point elasticity of copper export demand (2) would certainly increase in this process, there remains a strong impression that monopoly power is not fully exploited in the base year. In the model, pure profits are denied by imposing constant returns to scale, i.e. the contribution of improved Terms of Trade to GDP is not impaired.

Second, a rather large residual real income effect remains to be accounted for by the two other distortions included in the model: static labour cost differentials and import protection. For decomposing, structural change in employment and thus also in output must be considered first. Sectoral solutions presented in Table 2 are both the direct result of export taxes and subsidies and the indirect result of an appreciation of the real exchange rate (6.74 per cent) caused by real income growth. The diversification policy does not simply increase activity in other international sectors at the expense of copper mining. The appreciation fosters employment in services, it furthermore lowers relative prices of imported goods. Net sectoral effects then depend on trade shares. High export shares in domestic production and low import shares in domestic consumption give occasion to strong expansions in other mining and in export oriented light manufacturing, whereas the reverse constellation hinders entrepreneurs in import competing light manufacturing to take advantage of export subsidies. Contraction of heavy manufacturing employment is due to both falling prices of imports which account for 49 per cent of domestic consumption and to the withholding of export subsidies.

Static labour cost differentials have an impact on model solutions, since average wages per employed differ between sectors and the intersectoral wage ratios are kept constant. As wages per employed in contracting sectors (copper mining, export

---

17) Corden, W.M. 1974, p. 169.

manufacturing), however, are near the economy-wide average and labour moves into above- as well as below-average wage sectors, restructuring of employment carries no efficiency gains. Weighted by the economy-wide value added share of labour (41 per cent), there is even a small real income loss of about 0.02 per cent. The positive residual income effect must thus be attributed to the effect of compensating for current import protection and for the overvaluation of the exchange rate implied by it. Specifically, the highest protection is granted to heavy manufacturing both directly by tariffs and indirectly by the undervaluation of imported intermediates.

## 4.2 Instability under Flexible Exchange Rates

In experiment 2 the authorities are assumed to direct domestic credit at the employment target. As real income drops by 4.50 per cent following the copper price shock also money demand is shrinking. The simulation result shows that in order to achieve the real wage decline necessary for constant employment, the price level must be allowed to rise by 3.17 per cent against the expected inflation rate. Domestic credit supply, accordingly, must not be adjusted to the lower demand for money.

The structural change required for balancing the current account and employing all labour dismissed from copper mining is brought about by the currency depreciation of 8.19 per cent. After domestic inflation this is translated into a real exchange rate devaluation of 5.02 per cent stimulating non-copper exports and contracting all imports. Employment is reduced in the commodity and in the domestic sector, that is copper mining and services. All manufacturing sectors gain in employment as do agriculture and other mining. Export oriented sectors (other mining, export oriented light manufacturing) expand more than import substituting sectors as the price elasticities of export demand are substantially above those of import demand.

Large changes in sectoral labour demand may raise some

doubts as to whether supply is flexible enough to ensure constant aggregate employment. In semi-industrial countries a high percentage of total workforce is known to be waiting or searching for work at any time.[18] Additional labour demand can be met to some extent by workers living on the location. Structural employment instability rather makes the search for work even more attractive and thereby increases the rate of natural unemployment. Sectoral dismissals and hirings have been aggregated in Table 2 in order to provide an indicator for structural instability. As contraction or expansion of sectoral labour demand are determined by trade and cost structures, and the model has been disaggregated homogeneously in this respect, the indicator is unbiased. 2.99 per cent of labour force are dismissed from work and an equal percentage are hired.

Provided an export tax-cum-subsidy policy had led to the structural changes described in experiment 1, the copper price change would less affect the inflation rate (2.47 per cent) and would require a smaller amount of work-place switching (5.37 per cent) for keeping aggregate employment constant. Employment in the copper mining sector, however, is shown to be more sensitive to copper price changes, as diversification has lowered the production share of labour in copper mining. Adjusting factor inputs to output changes now requires a higher rate of change in the employment of the variable factor than before.

A flexible exchange rate regime encourages private diversification. As sectoral capital-stocks are fixed in the short-run closures of the model, the structure of employment changes also gives an indication of the structure of changes in return to capital. Private investors can reduce the variance in expected returns by expanding investment in export oriented sectors other than copper mining. Since this process has not been included in the model, the solutions both with and without the export-

---

18) See Berry, A. and R.H. Sabot 1978. In Chile the unemployment rate reached a low of 12 per cent in 1980-81 before the economic depression began.

cum-subsidy overstate the instability under flexible exchange rates.

## 4.3 Opportunity Costs of Stabilization under Fixed Exchange Rates

In the third experiment, the nominal exchange rate is defended against falling copper prices, and expansionary policies are implemented to cut the link between real income and real domestic absorption. The benefits of demand management under fixed rates, if successful, are shown by the solutions. The disturbance is contained within the commodity sector. There is only a slight decrease in the price level as credit expansion almost compensates for the difference between a contracting foreign component of money supply and shrinking money demand. Aggregate unemployment is mainly due to lay-offs in copper mining. Dismissals and hirings affect only 1.71 per cent of labour force. As also returns to capital are stabilized outside the copper sector, incentives for portfolio diversification are much reduced.

Costs arise from the necessity to finance a current account deficit of 634 Mill. US Dollar or 5.5 per cent of GDP as imports and non-copper exports remain almost unchanged after the copper price decline. If the authorities keep an additional average reserve stock for balancing the variations on current account induced by commodity export earnings, the society will have to bear the opportunity costs of returns foregone from alternative uses - like, for example, from investments into the domestic fixed capital stock or from smaller long-run debt commitments to international financial markets. As interest on these debts is higher than the interest that can be earned by holding the reserve in short-run foreign securities (for example in US treasury bills), the opportunity costs are positive.

The policy of export diversification cannot add to the stability of the macroeconomic variables as real domestic absorption has been fixed in both experiments with and without the structural change. The higher sensitivity of employment in the copper sector due to diversification even increases slightly the remaining instabilities. Reserve requirements fall to 562 Mill. US Dollars. Evaluating the opportunity costs of holding additional reserves with the interest rate differential between the country's long-run debt commitments and US treasury bills - about 3.6 per cent in the average between 1975 and 1980[19] - and comparing results, it becomes obvious that only a small cost reduction (2.6 Mill. US Dollars) is achieved. The main benefits of diversification are lying elsewhere.

## 4.4 Instability under Fixed Exchange Rates

Defending the nominal exchange rate against a deteriorating copper price without being equipped or willing to finance a deficit in the current account, the authorities must put up with a heavy contraction in domestic absorption. The solutions of experiment 4, in which this case is simulated, can be interpreted most conveniently in comparison with those of experiment 2 simulating the case of employment stabilization under flexible rates. Shrinking money supply now takes down the domestic price level by 4.50 per cent below the inflation rate expected in long-run equilibrium. Instead of a real wage decline by 3.17 per cent as required for constant aggregate employment, the claim is unintendedly increased by deflation. Employment consequently falls 7.18 per cent below the natural rate.

Fixing the nominal rate has only a minor stabilizing effect on the real exchange rate (-4.50 per cent instead of -5.02 per cent under flexible rates). Comparing structural results of both experiments, it can thus be seen that employment losses are distributed over all sectors, i.e. expansionary movements are

19) World Bank 1981, pp. 130-132. International Monetary Fund 1982.

mitigated and contractionary movements aggravated. This shifts the instability from sectors expanding on behalf of the real exchange rate devaluation to those contracting, i.e. from the international sectors to both the commodity and the domestic sector. In industries producing traded goods except copper, export expansion and import displacement are impaired by a shrinking domestic demand. In the mainly import competing sectors, the net employment effect even turns negative. Consequently, there is less incentive for diversifying investments in favour of the production of traded goods other than copper. Finally, with labour intensity in the domestic sector on average higher than in the international sectors - the value added share of labour is .46 in services but only .35 in the rest of the economy - shifting employment instability to the domestic sectors increases structural instability in total. Following the model simulation, 8.05 per cent instead of 5.98 per cent of labour force move either in or out of work places. Waiting and searching for work becomes more rewarding.

The export tax-cum-subsidy policy cuts down costs of defending the nominal exchange rate. Since total export earnings fluctuate less heavily, a balanced current account requires smaller changes in absorption. In the worst case, the domestic price level falls by 3.37 instead of by 4.50 per cent. A less volatile real exchange rate implies a smaller amount of hirings and dismissals: 6.49 instead of 8.05 per cent of the labour force are involved. Still, comparing fixed to flexible exchange rate solutions in the diversified economy, the instability of all variables but the nominal exchange rate - aggregate employment, domestic price level, structural employment - turns out smaller in the case of flexible exchange rates.

## 5. Summary and Conclusions

Instability of world commodity markets brings about macroeconomic disturbances in a group of countries earning their foreign exchange to substantial parts by exporting just a few primary commodities. The authorities of such countries can stabilize aggregate employment against external shocks by reserving monetary policies for that purpose, allowing the currency to find its price in the foreign exchange market. Export earnings fluctuations, however, will then cause domestic price level and sectoral employment fluctuations. Such adverse implications could be avoided within a fixed exchange rate regime, if the authorities were to succeed with attempts to stabilize real domestic absorption.

Fixing the nominal exchange rate, however, market incentives for export diversification are subdued as no longer do returns to capital vary inversely between sectors producing the commodity as well as non-traded goods on the one side and other international sectors on the other side. Less diversified, the economy is then exposed to wider export earnings fluctuations and to greater risks of shifting commodity price trends. The authorities might substitute export taxes-cum-subsidies for the market incentives in order to temper swings in earnings and regain security.

In the first experiment it was shown that a marginal export tax-cum-subsidy policy has a positive welfare effect irrespective of the instability and uncertainty issue. Real income is increasing. The result was crudely decomposed into a monopoly and an import protection effect, i.e. the measures turned out as solutions to current distortions. It follows that the instability of domestic variables is in part due to domestic distortions. Correcting for such distortions first, excess demand for price level and structural employment stability would be reduced. The case for stabilizing within a fixed exchange rate regime is then less convincing.

In the second experiment some implications of aggregate employment stabilization within a flexible exchange rate regime were quantified first within the undiversified economy. The solutions revealed that domestic price level and structural employment instability would indeed be high in such a case. Price level instability, however, is remarkably reduced already by the marginal diversification obtained in experiment 1. It must be kept in mind, furthermore, that portfolio diversification is not included in the model, i.e. the economy of the model is less diversified than after a period of adjustment to a flexible exchange rate regime. The indicators, therefore, overstate the instability relative to the fixed exchange rate cases.

In the third experiment, the authorities defend the exchange rate and stabilize real domestic absorption - relying on a stock of reserves built up for that purpose. Domestic price level, aggregate and structural employment can, as the model results confirm, indeed be stabilized to a large extent. Diversification would in such case have only little additional effect besides reducing the risk of stabilizing with respect to erroneous price projections. Opportunity costs of reserve-holding are reduced but by a small amount. In spite of high reserves, however, doubts persist whether the authorities of commodity-exporting countries can avoid speculative capital movements in face of drastic changes in the balance of current account after a copper price shock.

In the fourth experiment, therefore, the implications of defending the exchange rate without financing a current account deficit were examined. External equilibrium must then be obtained by massive deflation including a dramatic decline of employment. Both price level and structural employment stability are shown to be higher than in the case of flexible rates. By reducing fluctuations in export earnings, the export tax-cum-subsidy measure mitigates each of these adverse effects. In each case, however, the instability remains higher than under a flexible exchange rate system, in which monetary instruments are reserved for aggregate employment stabilization.

The task of determining the structural effects of a complete removal or correction of distortions has not been taken up here. Nor was private reaction to uncertainty included in the model. The quantitative results of this study nevertheless lead to the conclusion that the case for reacting to export earnings fluctuations by stabilization within a fixed exchange rate regime is not a strong one.

Finally, the paper has illustrated how a formal economy-wide framework can be used to assist policy makers in evaluating the implications of alternative proposed policies. As with all studies of an applied nature the results are conditional on (a) the numerous assumptions underlying the economic structure of the model used, and (b) the quality of the data used to specify the model numerically. The assumptions have been made explicit, as far as is possible, to enable the reader to judge their relevance. With respect to data, no effort has been made to assess the quality of the published sources. Least defendable, probably, is the assumption of a constant export demand elasticity in the case of an export diversification policy. The elasticity is more likely to increase thus removing the possibility of exploiting monopoly power. Note, however, that the monopoly effect accounted for the smaller part of the positive income result only. The compensation for trade distortions or the direct removal of these distortions will nevertheless lead to both higher real income and a more diversified economy. The beneficial effects of such diversification under commodity market instability have been worked out quantitatively. While the numerical projections have obvious limitations, they assist in arriving at the dimensions of policies required to cope with the external shock given specified targets.

References:

Adams, F.G., J.R. Behrman, Commodity Exports and Economic Development. The Commodity Problem and Policy in Developing Countries. Lexington, Mass. 1982.

Behrman, J.R., "Sectoral Elasticities of Substitution Between Capital and Labour in a Developing Economy: Time Series Analysis in the Case of Postwar Chile". Econometrica, Vol. 40 (1972).

Berry, A., R.H. Sabot, "Labour Market Performance in Developing Countries. A Survey". World Development, Vol. 6 (1978).

Corbo, V. and P. Meller, "La sustitución de trabajo, capital humano y capital fîsico en la industria manufacherera chilena". Estudios de Economîa, No. 14, 1979.

Dick, H., E. Gerken, T. Mayer, D. Vincent, "Stabilization Strategies in Primary Commodity Exporting Countries: A Case Study of Chile". Journal of Development Economics. Forthcoming.

Dixon, P.B., B.R. Parmenter, J. Sutton, D.P. Vincent, ORANI: A Multisectoral Model of the Australian Economy. Amsterdam 1982.

Gerken, E., Arbeitsmärkte in Entwicklungsländern. Tübingen 1981.

Gerken, E., "Stabilizing the Domestic Price Level under Fluctuating Terms of Trade". Working Paper No. 179, Kiel Institute of World Economics, June 1983.

Heller, H.R. and M.S. Khan, "The Demand for International Reserves under Fixed and Floating Exchange Rates". IMF Staff Papers, Vol. 25 (1978).

International Monetary Fund, International Financial Statics, 1982.

Johansen, L., A Multisectoral Study of Economic Growth. Amsterdam 1960.

Lasaga, M., The Copper Industry in the Chilean Economy. Lexington 1981.

Phelps, E.S., Inflation Policy and Unemployment Theory. The Cost-Benefit Approach to Monetary Planning. New York 1972.

Powell, Alan A., "The Major Streams of Economy-wide Modelling: Is Rapprochement Possible?" In: J. Kmenta and J.B. Ramsey (Eds.), Large Scale Econometric Models: Theory and Practice, North-Holland Publishing Company, Amsterdam 1982.

Presidencia de la República, Oficina de Planificación Nacional, Matriz de Insumo - Producto De La Economía chilena 1977. Santiago de Chile.

República de Chile, Instituto Nacional de Estadîsticas, Encuesta Nacional del Empleo. Santiago de Chile.

Taborga, M., Estructura De Consumo y Grupo Social. Departamento de Economía, Universidad de Chile, Santiago de Chile 1978.

Tanzi, V., M.J. Blejer, "Inflation, Interest Rate Policy, and Currency Substitutions in Developing Economies: A Discussion of Some Major Issues". World Development, Vol. 10 (1982).

Vincent, D.P., "Exchange Rates, Monetary Policy and Wages: A Case Study of Chile". Working Paper No. 164, Kiel Institute of World Economics, January 1983.

World Bank, Price Prospects for Major Primary Commodities. Report No. 814/80, 1980.

World Bank, World Debt Tables. External Public Debt of Developing Countries and Territories. EC-167/81, 1981.

World Bank, World Development Report 1982, 1982.

Table A1 The Chilean Model Equations: A Linear System in Percentage Changes[1]

| Identifier | Equation [2,3] | Subscript Range | Number | Description |
|---|---|---|---|---|
| | 1. Final Demands | | | |
| (1) | $x_{is}^{(3)} = x_i^{(3)} - \sigma_i^{(3)}(p_{is} - \sum_{s=1}^{2} S_{is}^{(3)} p_{is})$ | i=1,...,g<br>s=1,2 | 2g | Household demands for commodities by source |
| (2) | $x_i^{(3)} = q + \varepsilon_i(c - q) + \sum_{k=1}^{g} \eta_{ik} p_k$ | i=1,...,g | g | Household demands for commodities undifferentiated by source |
| (3) | $x_{(is)j}^{(2)} = y_j - \sigma_{ij}^{(2)}(p_{is} - \sum_{s=1}^{2} S_{(is)j}^{(2)} p_{is})$ | i=1,...,g<br>s=1,2<br>j=1,...,h | 2gh | Demands for inputs to capital creation |
| (4) | $x_{is}^{(5)} = c_R$ | i=1,...,g<br>s=1,2 | 2g | Other (mainly government) demands |
| (5) | $p_i^e = - \gamma_i x_{i1}^{(4)} + f_{i1}^{(4)}$ | i=1,...,g | g | Export demands |
| | 2. Industry Inputs | | | |
| (6) | $x_{(is)j}^{(1)} = z_j - \sigma_{ij}^{(1)}(p_{is} - \sum_{s=1}^{2} S_{(is)j}^{(1)} p_{is})$ | i=1,...,g<br>s=1,2<br>j=1,...,h | 2gh | Demands for intermediate inputs |
| (7) | $x_{vj}^P = z_j - \sigma_j^P (p_{vj}^P - \sum_{v=2}^{3} S_{vj} p_{vj}^P - S_{1j} p_1^P)$ | v=2,3<br>j=1,...,h | 2h | Demands for fixed capital (v=2) and land (v=3) |
| (8) | $x_{1j}^P = z_j - \sigma_j^P (p_1^P - \sum_{v=2}^{3} S_{vj} p_{vj}^P - S_{1j} p_1^P)$ | j=1,...,h | h | Demands for aggregate labour |
| (9) | $x_{1,q,j}^P = x_{1j}^P - \sigma_{1,j}^P (p_{1,q}^P - \sum_{q=1}^{r} S_{1,q,j} p_{1,q}^P$ | q=1,...,r<br>j=1,...,h | rh | Demands for labour of each occupation |
| | 3. Zero Pure Profits Conditions | | | |
| (10) | $p_{j1} = \sum_{i=1}^{g} \sum_{s=1}^{2} H_{(is)j}^{(1)} p_{is} + \sum_{q=1}^{r} H_{1,q,j}^P p_{1,q}^P$<br>$+ \sum_{v=2}^{3} H_{vj}^P p_{vj}^P + H_j^T p_{j1}$ | j=1,...,h | h | - in production |
| (11) | $\pi_j = \sum_{i=1}^{g} \sum_{s=1}^{2} H_{(is)j}^{(2)} p_{is}$ | j=1,...,h | h | - in capital creation |
| (12) | $p_{i2} = p_{i2}^m + t_i + \phi$ | i=1,...,h | g | - in importing |
| (13) | $p_{i1} = p_i^e + v_i + \phi$ | i=1,...,g | g | - in exporting |
| | 4. Market Clearing | | | Supply equals demand for |
| (14) | $z_j = \sum_{j=1}^{h} B_{(i1)j}^{(1)} x_{(i1)j}^{(1)} + \sum_{j=1}^{h} B_{(i1)j}^{(2)} x_{(i1)j}^{(2)}$<br>$+ B_{i1}^{(3)} x_{i1}^{(3)} + B_{i1}^{(4)} x_{i1}^{(4)} + B_{i1}^{(5)} x_{i1}^{(5)}$ | j=1,...,g | g | - domestically produced commodities |
| (15) | $\ell_q = \sum_{j=1}^{h} B_{1,q,j} x_{1,q,j}^P$ | q=1,...,r | r | - labour of each occupation |
| (16) | $k_j = x_{2j}^P$ | j=1,...,h | h | - capital |
| (17) | $n_j = x_{3j}^P$ | j=1,...,h | h | - land |

Table A1 continued The Chilean Model Equations: A Linear System in Percentage Changes [1]

| Identifier | Equation | Subscript Range | Number | Description |
|---|---|---|---|---|
| | 5. Miscellaneous | | | |
| (18) | $x_{i2} = \sum_{j=1}^{h} B^{(1)}_{(i2)j}\, x^{(1)}_{(i2)j} + \sum_{j=1}^{h} B^{(2)}_{(i2)j}\, x^{(2)}_{(i2)j}$ | | | |
| | $B^{(3)}_{i2}\, x^{(3)}_{i2} + B^{(5)}_{i2}\, x^{(5)}_{i2}$ | i=1,...,g | g | Competitive import volume |
| (19) | $m = \sum_{i=1}^{g} (p^{m}_{i2} + x_{i2})\, M_{i2}$ | | 1 | Foreign currency imports |
| (20) | $e = \sum_{i=1}^{g} (p^{e}_{i1} + x^{(4)}_{i1})\, E_{i1}$ | | 1 | Foreign currency exports |
| (21) | $100\Delta R = Ee - Mm$ | | 1 | Balance of current account |
| (22) | $r_j = Q_j\,(p^{P}_{2j} - \pi_j)$ | j=1,...,h | h | Rate of return to capital |
| (23) | $y_j = k_j + B_j\,(r_j - \lambda)$ | j=1,...,h | h | Industry investment |
| (24) | $\Sigma_j(\pi_j + y_j)T_j = i$ | | 1 | Investment budget (nominal) |
| (25) | $p^{P}_{1} = \sum_{q=1}^{r} p_{1,q}\, S_{1,q}$ | | 1 | Price of labour in general |
| (26) | $p_k = \sum_{s=1}^{2} S^{(3)}_{ks}\, p_{ks}$ | k=1,...,g | g | General price of goods to households |
| (27) | $\varepsilon^{(3)} = \sum_{i=1}^{g} \sum_{s=1}^{2} W^{(3)}_{is}\, p_{is}$ | | 1 | Consumer price index |
| (28) | $\varepsilon^{(2)} = \sum_{j=1}^{h} T_j\, \pi_j$ | | 1 | Capital goods price index |
| (29) | $c_R = c - \varepsilon^{(3)}$ | | 1 | Aggregate real consumption |
| (30) | $i_R = i - \varepsilon^{(2)}$ | | 1 | Aggregate real investment |
| (31) | $i_R = c_R$ | | 1 | Relationship between real consumption and investment |
| (32) | $\ell = \sum_{q=1}^{r} \ell_q\, \psi_{1q}$ | | 1 | Aggregate employment |
| (33) | $\kappa = \sum_{j=1}^{h} k_j\, \psi_{2j}$ | | 1 | Aggregate capital stock |
| (34) | $p^{P}_{1,q} = f_1$ | | r | Allows for exogenous setting of wages |
| (35) | $gdp = S_c c_R + S_i i_R + S_g \left( \sum_{s=1}^{2} \sum_{i=1}^{g} x^{(5)}_{is}\, S^{(5)}_{is} \right)$ | | 1 | |
| | $+ S_e e - S_m m$ | | | Gross domestic product |

Total equations = 4gh + 11g + 9h + rh + 2r + 13

1) The variables and coefficients are defined in Tables A2 and A3.

2) The model distinguishes 8 domestic industries each producing its respective commodity i.e., g and h = 8. Hence $p_{j1} = p_{i1}$, j = 1,...,h, i = 1,...,g. (Labels for these are given in Table 1). The labour market is divided into two occupational categories, i.e., r = 2. The superscript s denotes the source of the commodity, s = 1 (domestically produced), s = 2 (imported). The superscript v denotes the type of primary factor; v = 1 (aggregate labour), v = 2 (fixed capital), v = 3 (land).

3) The nomenclature of variable superscripts is as follows. Superscript "P" denotes a primary factor quantity or price, superscript "m" a foreign price for imports (cif) and superscript "e" a foreign price for exports (fob). Superscript (1) denotes the use of that variable in current production, (2) in capital creation, (3) by households, (4) exports and (5) by other (mainly government) demands. Note that there is no superscript on the local prices of domestic and imported commodities (the $p_{is}$). That is, the price of a commodity is assumed to be the same in all domestic end uses.

Table A2 Chilean Model Variables

| Variable [1] | Number | Description [2] |
|---|---|---|
| $x_{is}^{(3)}$ | 2g | Household demands for domestic and imported goods |
| $x_i^{(3)}$ | g | Household demands for goods undifferentiated by source |
| $p_{is}$ | 2g | Price of good i from source s |
| q | 1 | Number of households |
| c | 1 | Aggregate nominal household expenditure |
| $P_k$ | g | Price of consumer goods by type but not by source |
| $x_{(is)j}^{(2)}$ | 2gh | Demands for inputs (domestic and imported) for capital creation |
| $y_j$ | h | Capital creation by using industry |
| $x_{is}^{(5)}$ | 2g | Other (mainly government) demands for domestic and imported goods |
| $c_R$ | 1 | Aggregate real household expenditure |
| $P_i^e$ | g | F.o.b. foreign currency export prices |
| $x_{i1}^{(4)}$ | g | Export demands |
| $f_{i1}^{(4)}$ | g | Export demand shift variable |
| $x_{(is)j}^{(1)}$ | 2gh | Demands for inputs (domestic and imported) for current production |
| $z_j$ | h | Industry outputs |
| $x_{vj}^P$ | 3h | Industry demands for labour in general, fixed capital and land |
| $P_{vj}^P$ | 2h | Rental prices of capital (v=2) and land (v=3) in each industry |
| $P_1^P$ | 1 | Economy wide price of labour in general |
| $x_{1,q,j}^P$ | rh | Demands for labour by occupation and industry |
| $P_{1,q}^P$ | r | Price of labour by occupation |
| $\pi_j$ | h | Costs of units of capital |
| $P_{i2}^m$ | g | C.i.f. foreign currency prices for competing imports |
| $t_i$ | g | One plus the ad valorem rates of protection on imports |
| $\phi$ | 1 | Exchange rate (Chilean peso/foreign currency ($ US)) |
| $v_i$ | g | One plus ad valorem rates of export subsidies |
| $\ell_q$ | r | Employment by occupation |
| $k_j$ | h | Industry capital stocks |
| $n_j$ | h | Industry land |

Table A2 continued Chilean Model Variables

| Variable[1] | Number | Description[2] |
|---|---|---|
| $\varepsilon^{(3)}$ | 1 | Consumer price index |
| gdp | 1 | Gross domestic product |
| $\Delta R$ | 1 | Balance of current account |
| $x_{i2}$ | g | Commodity import volumes |
| m | 1 | Foreign currency value of imports |
| e | 1 | Foreign currency value of exports |
| $r_j$ | h | Industry rates of return to capital |
| $\lambda$ | 1 | Economy-wide expected rate of return |
| i | 1 | Aggregate nominal investment |
| $\varepsilon^{(2)}$ | 1 | Investment goods price index |
| $i_R$ | 1 | Aggregate real investment |
| $\ell$ | 1 | Aggregate employment |
| $\kappa$ | 1 | Economy's aggregate capital stock |
| $f_1$ | 1 | Shift term for economy-wide wage |

Total variables: $4gh + 15g + 11h + rh + 2r + 17$

1) The variable subscript range is as follows: $i,k = 1,\ldots,g$; $s = 1,2$; $v = 1,2,3$; $j = 1,\ldots,h$; $q = 1,\ldots r$.

2) All variables are in percentage changes except the balance of current account, $\Delta R$, which, because it can move through zero, is expressed in first differences.

Table A3 Coefficients of the Chilean Model

$\sigma_i^{(3)}$ $\sigma_{ij}^{(1)}$ $\sigma_{ij}^{(2)}$ CES import-domestic substitution elasticities for good i in household consumption ($\sigma_i^{(3)}$), intermediate usage in industry j for current production ($\sigma_{ij}^{(1)}$), and as inputs to capital creation ($\sigma_{ij}^{(2)}$). A common value of 2.0 was assigned to all these elasticities. This value, while judgemental, is consistent with estimates from the few published studies in this area.

$\sigma_j^P$ $\sigma_{1,j}^P$ CES substitution elasticities among primary factors ($\sigma_j^P$), and amongst occupational labour ($\sigma_{1,j}^P$) in industry j. Since relative wages between occupations were assumed fixed in all experiments the values assigned to $\sigma_{1,j}^P$ (1.0 for all j), exert no influence on the results. The following values for $\sigma_j^P$ were used, 1. Agriculture (0.31), 2. Copper mining (0.20), 3. Other mining (0.51), 4. Food processing (1.0), 5. Light manufacturing (import competing) (1.0), 6. Light manufacturing (export oriented) (1.0), 7. Heavy manufacturing (1.0), 8. Services (0.43). The values for sectors 1,3 and 8 were drawn from the econometric estimates in Behrman (1972), the value for sector 2 from the supply elasticity reported in Lasaga (1981). Values for the remaining sectors are based on the estimates reported in Corbo and Meller (1979).

$\varepsilon_i$ $\eta_{ik}$ Expenditure ($\varepsilon_i$) and cross price ($\eta_{ik}$ $i \neq k$) elasticities in household consumption for good i. Estimates for $\varepsilon_i$ were obtained from the Chilean household demand studies reported in Lluch, Powell and Williams (1977) and Taborga (1978).The estimates used for each of the eight commodity groups are, 1. (0.60), 2.-4. (0.75), 5. (1.10), 6. (1.41), 7. (1.62), 8. (1.18). Since the underlying household utility functions are assumed to be additive, the matrix of uncompensated own price ($\eta_{ii}$) and cross price ($\eta_{ik}$) consumer demand elasticities were obtained from

Table A3 continued Coefficients of the Chilean Model

$$\eta_{ii} = \frac{\varepsilon_i}{w} - \varepsilon_i \alpha_i \left(1 + \frac{\varepsilon_i}{w}\right)$$

$$\eta_{ik} = - \varepsilon_i \alpha_j \left(1 + \frac{\varepsilon_j}{w}\right) \qquad i \neq k$$

Where w is the Frisch parameter and $\alpha_j$ are household budget shares calculated from the 1977 input output table. The estimate of w (-2.525) was obtained using the relationship between per capita GDP and Frisch parameter values estimated by Lluch, Powell and Williams (1977).

$\gamma_i$ Reciprocals of the foreign demand elasticities for Chilean export commodity i. For all commodity categories except copper, the "small country" assumption was approximated by assigning a small value (0.05) to the respective $\gamma_i$'s. For copper, a value of 0.5 was used. This value is based principally on the world price elasticity of demand for copper and the Chilean share in world copper exports.

$Q_j$ $B_j$ $T_j$ Industry investment parameters. $Q_j$ is the ratio of the gross (before depreciation) to the net (after depreciation) rate of return in industry j. $B_j$ is the reciprocal of the elasticity of the expected rate of return schedule for industry j times the ratio of its gross investment to its following year capital stock. $T_j$ is the share of total investment accounted for by industry j. $T_j$ was obtained from the 1977 Chilean input-output table. $Q_j$ and $B_j$ are judgemental.

$\psi_{1q}$ $\psi_{2j}$ Respectively the share of aggregate employment accounted for by occupation q and the share of the economy's aggregate capital stock in industry j. The percentage share of skilled (52.2) and unskilled (47.8) workers was obtained from República de Chile, encuesta nacional del empleo. Values for $\psi_{2j}$ were calculated by using information given in the 1977 Chilean input-output table.

Table A3 continued Coefficients of the Chilean Model

| | |
|---|---|
| $S_c$<br>$S_i$<br>$S_g$<br>$S_c$<br>$S_m$ | Respectively the shares of GDP accounted for by aggregate consumption, investment, other (mainly government) domestic, export and import demand. The shares, which sum to unity, were obtained from the 1977 Chilean input-output table. |
| $S^{(1)}_{(is)j}$<br>$S^{(2)}_{(is)j}$ | Shares of good i from source s (domestic or imported) in industry j's purchases of i for current production (1), and capital creation (2). Obtained from the 1977 Chilean input- output table. |
| $S^{(3)}_{is}$ | Share of the value of good i from source s in the total purchases of good i by households. Obtained from the 1977 Chilean input output table. |
| $S_{vj}$<br>$S_{1,q,j}$ | Respectively the share of primary factor v in the total primary factor costs of industry j and the share of labour by occupation q in industry j's total labour costs. Obtained from the 1977 Chilean input-output table. |
| $H^{(1)}_{(is)j}$<br>$H^{P}_{1,q,j}$<br>$H^{P}_{2j}$<br>$H^{P}_{3j}$<br>$H^{T}_{j}$ | Respectively the shares of industry j's production costs represented by intermediate inputs of good i from source s, labour inputs of occupation q,fixed capital,land, and net indirect taxes. Obtained from the 1977 Chilean input-output table. |
| $B^{(1)}_{(i1)j}$<br>$B^{(2)}_{(i1)j}$<br>$B^{(3)}_{i1}$<br>$B^{(4)}_{i1}$<br>$B^{(5)}_{i1}$ | Respectively the share of the total sales of domestic good i absorbed by, inputs to industry j for current production (1), and for capital creation (2), by households (3),exports (4), and other (mainly government) demands (5). Obtained from the 1977 Chilean input-output table. |

Table A3 continued Coefficients of the Chilean Model

| | |
|---|---|
| $B^{(1)}_{(i2)j}$ $B^{(2)}_{(i2)j}$ $B^{(3)}_{(i2)}$ $B^{(5)}_{i2}$ | Respectively the share of the total sales of imported good i absorbed by, inputs to industry j for current production (1) and for capital creation (2), by households (3), exports (4), and other (mainly government) demands (5). Obtained from the 1977 Chilean input-output table. |
| $B_{1,q,j}$ $S_{1,q}$ | Share of the economy's employment of occupation q accounted for in industry j, and cost share of labour of type q in the economy's total labour cost respectively. Obtained from the 1977 Chilean input-output table. |
| $S^{(5)}_{is}$ | Share of aggregate other demands accounted for by other demand for good i from source s. Obtained from the 1977 Chilean input-output table. |
| $M_{i2}$ $E_{i1}$ $M$ $E$ | The share of total foreign currency costs accounted for by imported good i ($M_{i2}$), the share of total foreign currency export earnings accounted for by exported commodity i ($E_{i1}$), the aggregate foreign currency value of imports (M), and the aggregate foreign currency value of exports (E). Obtained from the 1977 Chilean input-output table. |
| $W^{(3)}_{is}$ | Expenditure weight of good i from source s in the model's index of consumer prices. Obtained from the 1977 Chilean input-output table. |

Table A4 Exogenous Variable Selection and Values for Each Experiment

| Variable | Number | Experiment 1 | 2 | 3 | 4 |
|---|---|---|---|---|---|
| $r_j$ | h | 0 | | | |
| $k_j$ | h | | 0 | 0 | 0 |
| $n_j$ | h | 0 | 0 | 0 | 0 |
| q | 1 | 0 | 0 | 0 | 0 |
| $f_{i1}^{(4)}$ (i=1,3-8) | g-1 | 0 | 0 | 0 | 0 |
| $f_{i1}^{(4)}$ (i=2) | 1 | 0 | -41.37 | -41.37 | -41.37 |
| $p_{i2}^{m}$ | g | 0 | 0 | 0 | 0 |
| $t_i$ | g | 0 | 0 | 0 | 0 |
| $v_i$ (i=1,3-6) | g-3 | $\frac{10}{v_i}$ | 0 | 0 | 0 |
| $v_i$ (i=2) | 1 | $-\frac{10}{v_i}$ | 0 | 0 | 0 |
| $x_{i1}^{(4)}$ (i=7,8) | 2 | 0 | 0 | 0 | 0 |
| $f_1$ | 1 | | 0 | 0 | 0 |
| $\phi$ | 1 | 0 | | 0 | 0 |
| $c_R$ | 1 | | | 0 | |
| $\Delta R$ | 1 | 0 | 0 | | 0 |
| $\ell$ | 1 | 0 | 0 | | |

A set of 2g + (g-1) + h + 1 exogenous variables is common to all experiments, h + g + 4 further variables are specific for each experiment.

1) For variables labels see Table A2.

2) The model is allowed to explain exports for the major export commodities, i.e., those whose sales pattern is such that their domestic prices can be regarded as being set by their corresponding world prices. For other commodities, exports are determined exogenously with the model endogenising the corresponding export subsidy/tax variable. (Note from (13) that if $v_i$ is exogenous then $p_{i1}$ will tend to move with $p_i^e$. If $v_i$ is endogenous then $p_{i1}$ will move independently of $p_i^e$).

<u>Author Index</u>

Subject Index

Vol. 101: W. M. Wonham, Linear Multivariable Control. A Geometric Approach. X, 344 pages. 1974.

Vol. 102: Analyse Convexe et Ses Applications. Comptes Rendus, Janvier 1974. Edited by J.-P. Aubin. IV, 244 pages. 1974.

Vol. 103: D. E. Boyce, A. Farhi, R. Weischedel, Optimal Subset Selection. Multiple Regression, Interdependence and Optimal Network Algorithms. XIII, 187 pages. 1974.

Vol. 104: S. Fujino, A Neo-Keynesian Theory of Inflation and Economic Growth. V, 96 pages. 1974.

Vol. 105: Optimal Control Theory and its Applications. Part I. Proceedings 1973. Edited by B. J. Kirby. VI, 425 pages. 1974.

Vol. 106: Optimal Control Theory and its Applications. Part II. Proceedings 1973. Edited by B. J. Kirby. VI, 403 pages. 1974.

Vol. 107: Control Theory, Numerical Methods and Computer Systems Modeling. International Symposium, Rocquencourt, June 17–21, 1974. Edited by A. Bensoussan and J. L. Lions. VIII, 757 pages. 1975.

Vol. 108: F. Bauer et al., Supercritical Wing Sections II. A Handbook. V, 296 pages. 1975.

Vol. 109: R. von Randow, Introduction to the Theory of Matroids. IX, 102 pages. 1975.

Vol. 110: C. Striebel, Optimal Control of Discrete Time Stochastic Systems. III. 208 pages. 1975.

Vol. 111: Variable Structure Systems with Application to Economics and Biology. Proceedings 1974. Edited by A. Ruberti and R. R. Mohler. VI, 321 pages. 1975.

Vol. 112: J. Wilhelm, Objectives and Multi-Objective Decision Making Under Uncertainty. IV, 111 pages. 1975.

Vol. 113: G. A. Aschinger, Stabilitätsaussagen über Klassen von Matrizen mit verschwindenden Zeilensummen. V, 102 Seiten. 1975.

Vol. 114: G. Uebe, Produktionstheorie. XVII, 301 Seiten. 1976.

Vol. 115: Anderson et al., Foundations of System Theory: Finitary and Infinitary Conditions. VII, 93 pages. 1976

Vol. 116: K. Miyazawa, Input-Output Analysis and the Structure of Income Distribution. IX, 135 pages. 1976.

Vol. 117: Optimization and Operations Research. Proceedings 1975. Edited by W. Oettli and K. Ritter. IV, 316 pages. 1976.

Vol. 118: Traffic Equilibrium Methods, Proceedings 1974. Edited by M. A. Florian. XXIII, 432 pages. 1976.

Vol. 119: Inflation in Small Countries. Proceedings 1974. Edited by H. Frisch. VI, 356 pages. 1976.

Vol. 120: G. Hasenkamp, Specification and Estimation of Multiple-Output Production Functions. VII, 151 pages. 1976.

Vol. 121: J. W. Cohen, On Regenerative Processes in Queueing Theory. IX, 93 pages. 1976.

Vol. 122: M. S. Bazaraa, and C. M. Shetty, Foundations of Optimization VI. 193 pages. 1976

Vol. 123: Multiple Criteria Decision Making. Kyoto 1975. Edited by M. Zeleny. XXVII, 345 pages. 1976.

Vol. 124: M. J. Todd. The Computation of Fixed Points and Applications. VII, 129 pages. 1976.

Vol. 125: Karl C. Mosler. Optimale Transportnetze. Zur Bestimmung ihres kostengünstigsten Standorts bei gegebener Nachfrage. VI, 142 Seiten. 1976.

Vol. 126: Energy, Regional Science and Public Policy. Energy and Environment I. Proceedings 1975. Edited by M. Chatterji and P. Van Rompuy. VIII, 316 pages. 1976.

Vol. 127: Environment, Regional Science and Interregional Modeling. Energy and Environment II. Proceedings 1975. Edited by M. Chatterji and P. Van Rompuy. IX, 211 pages. 1976.

Vol. 128: Integer Programming and Related Areas. A Classified Bibliography. Edited by C. Kastning. XII, 495 pages. 1976.

Vol. 129: H.-J. Lüthi, Komplementaritäts- und Fixpunktalgorithmen in der mathematischen Programmierung. Spieltheorie und Ökonomie. VII, 145 Seiten. 1976.

Vol. 130: Multiple Criteria Decision Making, Jouy-en-Josas, France. Proceedings 1975. Edited by H. Thiriez and S. Zionts. VI, 409 pages. 1976.

Vol. 131: Mathematical Systems Theory. Proceedings 1975. Edited by G. Marchesini and S. K. Mitter. X, 408 pages. 1976.

Vol. 132: U. H. Funke, Mathematical Models in Marketing. A Collection of Abstracts. XX, 514 pages. 1976.

Vol. 133: Warsaw Fall Seminars in Mathematical Economics 1975. Edited by M. W. Loś, J. Loś, and A. Wieczorek. V. 159 pages. 1976.

Vol. 134: Computing Methods in Applied Sciences and Engineering. Proceedings 1975. VIII, 390 pages. 1976.

Vol. 135: H. Haga, A Disequilibrium – Equilibrium Model with Money and Bonds. A Keynesian – Walrasian Synthesis. VI, 119 pages. 1976.

Vol. 136: E. Kofler und G. Menges, Entscheidungen bei unvollständiger Information. XII, 357 Seiten. 1976.

Vol. 137: R. Wets, Grundlagen Konvexer Optimierung. VI, 146 Seiten. 1976.

Vol. 138: K. Okuguchi, Expectations and Stability in Oligopoly Models. VI, 103 pages. 1976.

Vol. 139: Production Theory and Its Applications. Proceedings. Edited by H. Albach and G. Bergendahl. VIII, 193 pages. 1977.

Vol. 140: W. Eichhorn and J. Voeller, Theory of the Price Index. Fisher's Test Approach and Generalizations. VII, 95 pages. 1976.

Vol. 141: Mathematical Economics and Game Theory. Essays in Honor of Oskar Morgenstern. Edited by R. Henn and O. Moeschlin. XIV, 703 pages. 1977.

Vol. 142: J. S. Lane, On Optimal Population Paths. V, 123 pages. 1977.

Vol. 143: B. Näslund, An Analysis of Economic Size Distributions. XV, 100 pages. 1977.

Vol. 144: Convex Analysis and Its Applications. Proceedings 1976. Edited by A. Auslender. VI, 219 pages. 1977.

Vol. 145: J. Rosenmüller, Extreme Games and Their Solutions. IV, 126 pages. 1977.

Vol. 146: In Search of Economic Indicators. Edited by W. H. Strigel. XVI, 198 pages. 1977.

Vol. 147: Resource Allocation and Division of Space. Proceedings. Edited by T. Fujii and R. Sato. VIII, 184 pages. 1977.

Vol. 148: C. E. Mandl, Simulationstechnik und Simulationsmodelle in den Sozial- und Wirtschaftswissenschaften. IX, 173 Seiten. 1977.

Vol. 149: Stationäre und schrumpfende Bevölkerungen: Demographisches Null- und Negativwachstum in Österreich. Herausgegeben von G. Feichtinger. VI, 262 Seiten. 1977.

Vol. 150: Bauer et al., Supercritical Wing Sections III. VI, 179 pages. 1977.

Vol. 151: C. A. Schneeweiß, Inventory-Production Theory. VI, 116 pages. 1977.

Vol. 152: Kirsch et al., Notwendige Optimalitätsbedingungen und ihre Anwendung. VI, 157 Seiten. 1978.

Vol. 153: Kombinatorische Entscheidungsprobleme: Methoden und Anwendungen. Herausgegeben von T. M. Liebling und M. Rössler. VIII, 206 Seiten. 1978.

Vol. 154: Problems and Instruments of Business Cycle Analysis. Proceedings 1977. Edited by W. H. Strigel. VI, 442 pages. 1978.

Vol. 155: Multiple Criteria Problem Solving. Proceedings 1977. Edited by S. Zionts. VIII, 567 pages. 1978.

Vol. 156: B. Näslund and B. Sellstedt, Neo-Ricardian Theory. With Applications to Some Current Economic Problems. VI, 165 pages. 1978.

Vol. 157: Optimization and Operations Research. Proceedings 1977. Edited by R. Henn, B. Korte, and W. Oettli. VI, 270 pages. 1978.

Vol. 158: L. J. Cherene, Set Valued Dynamical Systems and Economic Flow. VIII, 83 pages. 1978.

Vol. 159: Some Aspects of the Foundations of General Equilibrium Theory: The Posthumous Papers of Peter J. Kalman. Edited by J. Green. VI, 167 pages. 1978.

Vol. 160: Integer Programming and Related Areas. A Classified Bibliography. Edited by D. Hausmann. XIV, 314 pages. 1978.

Vol. 161: M. J. Beckmann, Rank in Organizations. VIII, 164 pages. 1978.

Vol. 162: Recent Developments in Variable Structure Systems, Economics and Biology. Proceedings 1977. Edited by R. R. Mohler and A. Ruberti. VI, 326 pages. 1978.

Vol. 163: G. Fandel, Optimale Entscheidungen in Organisationen. VI, 143 Seiten. 1979.

Vol. 164: C. L. Hwang and A. S. M. Masud, Multiple Objective Decision Making – Methods and Applications. A State-of-the-Art Survey. XII, 351 pages. 1979.

Vol. 165: A. Maravall, Identification in Dynamic Shock-Error Models. VIII, 158 pages. 1979.

Vol. 166: R. Cuninghame-Green, Minimax Algebra. XI, 258 pages. 1979.

Vol. 167: M. Faber, Introduction to Modern Austrian Capital Theory. X, 196 pages. 1979.

Vol. 168: Convex Analysis and Mathematical Economics. Proceedings 1978. Edited by J. Kriens. V, 136 pages. 1979.

Vol. 169: A. Rapoport et al., Coalition Formation by Sophisticated Players. VII, 170 pages. 1979.

Vol. 170: A. E. Roth, Axiomatic Models of Bargaining. V, 121 pages. 1979.

Vol. 171: G. F. Newell, Approximate Behavior of Tandem Queues. XI, 410 pages. 1979.

Vol. 172: K. Neumann and U. Steinhardt, GERT Networks and the Time-Oriented Evaluation of Projects. 268 pages. 1979.

Vol. 173: S. Erlander, Optimal Spatial Interaction and the Gravity Model. VII, 107 pages. 1980.

Vol. 174: Extremal Methods and Systems Analysis. Edited by A. V. Fiacco and K. O. Kortanek. XI, 545 pages. 1980.

Vol. 175: S. K. Srinivasan and R. Subramanian, Probabilistic Analysis of Redundant Systems. VII, 356 pages. 1980.

Vol. 176: R. Färe, Laws of Diminishing Returns. VIII, 97 pages. 1980.

Vol. 177: Multiple Criteria Decision Making-Theory and Application. Proceedings, 1979. Edited by G. Fandel and T. Gal. XVI, 570 pages. 1980.

Vol. 178: M. N. Bhattacharyya, Comparison of Box-Jenkins and Bonn Monetary Model Prediction Performance. VII, 146 pages. 1980.

Vol. 179: Recent Results in Stochastic Programming. Proceedings, 1979. Edited by P. Kall and A. Prékopa. IX, 237 pages. 1980.

Vol. 180: J. F. Brotchie, J. W. Dickey and R. Sharpe, TOPAZ – General Planning Technique and its Applications at the Regional, Urban, and Facility Planning Levels. VII, 356 pages. 1980.

Vol. 181: H. D. Sherali and C. M. Shetty, Optimization with Disjunctive Constraints. VIII, 156 pages. 1980.

Vol. 182: J. Wolters, Stochastic Dynamic Properties of Linear Econometric Models. VIII, 154 pages. 1980.

Vol. 183: K. Schittkowski, Nonlinear Programming Codes. VIII, 242 pages. 1980.

Vol. 184: R. E. Burkard and U. Derigs, Assignment and Matching Problems: Solution Methods with FORTRAN-Programs. VIII, 148 pages. 1980.

Vol. 185: C. C. von Weizsäcker, Barriers to Entry. VI, 220 pages. 1980.

Vol. 186: Ch.-L. Hwang and K. Yoon, Multiple Attribute Decision Making – Methods and Applications. A State-of-the-Art-Survey. XI, 259 pages. 1981.

Vol. 187: W. Hock, K. Schittkowski, Test Examples for Nonlinear Programming Codes. V. 178 pages. 1981.

Vol. 188: D. Bös, Economic Theory of Public Enterprise. VII, 142 pages. 1981.

Vol. 189: A. P. Lüthi, Messung wirtschaftlicher Ungleichheit. IX, 287 pages. 1981.

Vol. 190: J. N. Morse, Organizations: Multiple Agents with Multiple Criteria. Proceedings, 1980. VI, 509 pages. 1981.

Vol. 191: H. R. Sneessens, Theory and Estimation of Macroeconomic Rationing Models. VII, 138 pages. 1981.

Vol. 192: H. J. Bierens: Robust Methods and Asymptotic Theory in Nonlinear Econometrics. IX, 198 pages. 1981.

Vol. 193: J. K. Sengupta, Optimal Decisions under Uncertainty. VII, 156 pages. 1981.

Vol. 194: R. W. Shephard, Cost and Production Functions. XI, 104 pages. 1981.

Vol. 195: H. W. Ursprung, Die elementare Katastrophentheorie. Eine Darstellung aus der Sicht der Ökonomie. VII, 332 pages. 1982.

Vol. 196: M. Nermuth, Information Structures in Economics. VIII, 236 pages. 1982.

Vol. 197: Integer Programming and Related Areas. A Classified Bibliography. 1978 – 1981. Edited by R. von Randow. XIV, 338 pages. 1982.

Vol. 198: P. Zweifel, Ein ökonomisches Modell des Arztverhaltens. XIX, 392 Seiten. 1982.

Vol. 199: Evaluating Mathematical Programming Techniques. Proceedings, 1981. Edited by J.M. Mulvey. XI, 379 pages. 1982.

Vol. 200: The Resource Sector in an Open Economy. Edited by H. Siebert. IX, 161 pages. 1984.

# Ökonometrie und Unternehmensforschung
# Econometrics and Operations Research

GPSR Compliance

*The European Union's (EU) General Product Safety Regulation (GPSR) is a set of rules that requires consumer products to be safe and our obligations to ensure this.*

*If you have any concerns about our products, you can contact us on ProductSafety@springernature.com*

In case Publisher is established outside the EU, the EU authorized representative is:

Springer Nature Customer Service Center GmbH
Europaplatz 3
69115 Heidelberg, Germany

**Batch number: 10838062**

Printed by Printforce, the Netherlands